Non-Places

Non-Places

Introduction to an Anthropology
of Supermodernity

—————◆—————

MARC AUGÉ

Translated by
John Howe

VERSO

London · New York

This translation has been published with financial assistance from the French Ministère des Affaires Étrangères.

First published by Verso 1995
This edition © Verso 1995
Translation © John Howe 1995
Reprinted 1997, 1999, 2000
First published as *Non-Lieux, Introduction à une anthropologie de la surmodernité*
© Editions du Seuil 1992
All rights reserved

Verso
UK: 6 Meard Street, London W1V 3HR
USA: 180 Varick Street, New York, NY 10014

Verso is the imprint of New Left Books

ISBN 1–85984–956–3
ISBN 1–85984–051–5 (pbk)

British Library Cataloguing in Publication Data
A catalogue record for this book is available from the
British Library

Library of Congress Cataloging-in-Publication Data
Augé, Marc.
  [Non-lieux, English]
  Non-places : introduction to an anthropology of supermodernity /
Marc Augé ; translated by John Howe.
    p. cm.
  Includes bibliographical references.
  ISBN 1–85984–956–3. — ISBN 1–85984–051–5 (pbk.)
  1. Ethnology—Philosophy. 2. Space perception. I. Title.
GN345.A92513 1995
301'.01—dc20   94–46299
                                                      CIP

Typeset by M Rules
Printed and bound in Great Britain by
Biddles Ltd, www.biddles.co.uk

Contents

Prologue

On the way to his car Pierre Dupont stopped at the cash dispenser to draw some money. The device accepted his card and told him he could have 1800 francs. Pierre Dupont pressed the button beside this figure on the screen. The device asked him to wait a moment and then delivered the sum requested, reminding him as it did so to withdraw his card. 'Thank you for your custom,' it added as Pierre Dupont arranged the banknotes in his wallet.

It was a trouble-free drive, the trip to Paris on the A11 autoroute presenting no problems on a Sunday morning. There was no tailback at the junction where he joined it. He paid at the Dourdan tollbooth using his blue card, skirted Paris on the *périphérique* and took the A1 to Roissy.

He parked in row J of underground level 2, slid his parking ticket into his wallet and hurried to the Air France check-in desks. With some relief he deposited his suitcase (exactly 20 kilos) and handed his flight ticket to the hostess, asking if it would be possible to have a smoking seat next to the gangway. Silent and smiling, she assented with an inclination of her head, after first consulting her computer, then gave him back his ticket along with a boarding pass. 'Boarding from Satellite B at eighteen hundred,' she told him.

He went early through Passport Control to do a little duty-free shopping. He bought a bottle of cognac (something French for his Asian clients) and a box of cigars (for himself). Meticulously, he put the receipt away next to his blue card.

He strolled past the window-displays of luxury goods, glancing briefly at their jewellery, clothing and scent bottles, then called at the bookshop where he leafed through a couple of magazines before choosing an undemanding book: travel, adventure, spy fiction. Then he resumed his unhurried progress.

He was enjoying the feeling of freedom imparted by having got rid of his luggage and at the same time, more intimately, by the certainty that, now that he was 'sorted out', his identity registered, his boarding pass in his pocket, he had nothing to do but wait for the sequence of events. 'Roissy, just the two of us!': these days, surely, it was in these crowded places where thousands of individual itineraries converged for a moment, unaware of one another, that there survived something of the uncertain charm of the waste lands, the yards and building sites, the station platforms and waiting rooms where travellers break step, of all the chance meeting places where fugitive feelings occur of the possibility of continuing adventure, the feeling that all there is to do is to 'see what happens'.

The passengers boarded without problems. Those whose boarding passes bore the letter Z were requested to board last, and he observed with a certain amusement the muted, unnecessary jostling of the Xs and Ys around the door to the boarding gangway.

Waiting for take-off, while newspapers were being distributed, he glanced through the company's in-flight magazine and ran his finger along the imagined route of the journey: Heraklion, Larnaca, Beirut, Dhahran, Dubai, Bombay, Bangkok . . . more than nine thousand kilometres in the blink of an eye, and a few names which had cropped up in the news over the years. He cast his eye down the duty-free price list, noted that credit cards were accepted on intercontinental flights, and read with a certain smugness the advantages conferred by the 'business class' in which he was travelling thanks to the intelligent generosity of his firm ('At Charles de Gaulle 2 and New York, Club lounges are provided where you can rest, make telephone calls, use a photocopier or Minitel . . . . Apart from a personal welcome and constant attentive service, the new Espace 2000 seat has been designed for extra width and has separately adjustable backrest and headrest . . .'). He examined briefly the digitally labelled control panel of his Espace 2000 seat and then, drifting back into the advertisements in the magazine, admired the aerodynamic lines of a few late-model roadsters and gazed at the pictures of some large hotels belonging to an international chain, somewhat pompously described as 'the surroundings of civilization' (the Mammounia in Marrakesh, 'once a palace, now the quintessence of five-star luxury', the Brussels Métropole, 'where the splendours of the nineteenth century remain very much alive'). Then he came across an advertisement for a car with the same name as his seat, the Renault Espace: 'One day, the need for space makes itself felt . . . . It comes to us without warning. And never goes away. The irresistible wish for a space of our own. A mobile space which can take us anywhere. A space where everything is to hand and nothing is lacking . . . .' Just like the aircraft really. 'Already, space is inside you . . . . You've never been so firmly on the ground as you are in (the E)space,' the advertisement ended pleasingly.

★

They were taking off. He flicked rapidly through the
rest of the magazine, giving a few seconds to a piece on
'the hippopotamus – lord of the river' which began
with an evocation of Africa as 'cradle of legends' and
'continent of magic and sorcery'; glancing at an article
about Bologna ('You can be in love anywhere, but in
Bologna you fall in love with the city'). A brightly
coloured advertisement in English for a Japanese
'videomovie' held his attention for a moment ('Vivid
colors, vibrant sound and non-stop action. Make them
yours forever'). A Trenet song, heard that afternoon
over the car radio on the autoroute, had been running
through his head, and he mused that its line about the
'photo, the old photo of my youth' would soon
become meaningless to future generations. The colours
of the present preserved for ever: the camera as freezer.
An advertisement for the Visa card managed to reassure
him ('Accepted in Dubai and wherever you travel . . . .
Travel in full confidence with your Visa card').

He glanced distractedly through a few book
reviews, pausing for a moment on the review of a
work called *Euromarketing* which aroused his professional interest:

The homogenization of needs and consumption pat-
terns is one of the overall trends characterizing the new

international business environment . . . . Starting from
an examination of the effects of the globalization phenomenon on European business, on the validity and
content of Euromarketing and on predictable develop-
ments in the international marketing environment,
numerous issues are discussed.

The review ended with an evocation of 'the conditions suitable for the development of a mix that would
be as standardized as possible' and 'the architecture of
a European communication'.

Somewhat dreamily, Pierre Dupont put down his
magazine. The 'Fasten seat belt' notice had gone out.
He adjusted his earphones, selected Channel 5 and
allowed himself to be invaded by the adagio of Joseph
Haydn's Concerto No. 1 in E major. For a few hours
(the time it would take to fly over the Mediterranean,
the Arabian Sea and the Bay of Bengal), he would be
alone at last.

The Near and
the Elsewhere

More and more is being said about the anthropology
of the near. A seminar held in 1987 at the Musée des
Arts et Traditions populaires ('Social anthropology and
ethnology of France'), whose papers were published in
1989 under the title *L'Autre et le semblable*, noted a
convergence in the concerns of ethnologists working
elsewhere and those working here. Both the seminar
and the book are explicitly placed in the aftermath of
the reflections started at the Toulouse seminar of 1982
('New paths in the ethnology of France') and devel-
oped in a few books and special issues of reviews.

That said, it is by no means certain that (as is so

7

often the case) the recognition of new interests and fields for research, of hitherto unsuspected convergences, is not based at least partly on misunderstandings, or responsible for causing them. A few preliminary remarks may help to clarify this reflection on the anthropology of the near.

Anthropology has always dealt with the here and now. The practising ethnologist is a person situated somewhere (his 'here' of the moment) who describes what he is observing or what he is hearing at this very moment. It will always be possible afterwards to wonder about the quality of his observation and about the aims, prejudices or other factors that condition the production of his text: but the fact remains that all ethnology presupposes the existence of a direct witness to a present actuality. The theoretical anthropologist, who calls on observations and terrain other than his own, refers to observations that have been made by ethnologists, not to indirect sources which he would have to strive to interpret. Even the armchair anthropologist we all become from time to time is different from the historian who exploits a document. The facts we seek in Murdock's files[1] may have

---

1. This is a reference to George Peter Murdock's vast ethnographic survey, the 'Human Relations Area File', sometimes known simply as 'Murdock's files', a summary of which can be found in his *Outline of World Cultures*, New Haven, 1963. [Tr.]

been observed well or badly; but they have been observed, and in relation to elements (rules of alliance, of lineage, of inheritance) which also belong to 'second-degree' anthropology. Anything remote from direct observation of the terrain is also remote from anthropology; historians who take an interest in anthropology are still not anthropologists. The term 'historical anthropology' is ambiguous to say the least. 'Anthropological history' seems more appropriate. A symmetrical and inverse example might be found in the way anthropologists – Africanists, for example – are obliged to dip into history, notably in the form it has taken in the oral tradition. Everyone knows Hampaté Ba's dictum that in Africa an old person dying is 'a library on fire'; but the informant, whether old or not, is somebody having a conversation, who tells us less about the past than about what he knows or thinks about the past. He is not contemporary with the event he narrates, but the ethnologist is contemporary with both the narrative and the narrator. The informant's account says as much about the present as it does about the past. So the anthropologist, who has and ought to have historical interests, is nevertheless not *stricto sensu* a historian. These remarks are intended only to help define approaches and objects: obviously the work of historians like Ginzburg, Le Goff or Le Roy Ladurie is of the greatest interest to anthropologists. But it is still the work of historians, concerned with the past and derived from the study of documents.

So much for the 'now'. Let us move on to the 'here'. Certainly the European, Western 'here' assumes its full meaning in relation to the distant elsewhere – formerly 'colonial', now 'under-developed' – favoured in the past by British and French anthropology. But the opposition of here and elsewhere (a sort of gross division – Europe, rest of the world – reminiscent of the football matches organized by England in the days when it still had great football: England vs Rest of the World) can serve as a starting point for the opposition of the two anthropologies only by presupposing the very thing that is in question: that they are indeed two distinct anthropologies.

The assertion that ethnologists are turning to Europe as overseas fieldwork becomes more difficult to arrange is an arguable one. In the first place, there are still ample opportunities to work abroad, in Africa, Asia and the Americas . . . . In the second place, the reasons for doing anthropological work in Europe are positive ones. It is not a matter of second best, an anthropology by default. And it is precisely by examining these positive reasons that we may come to question the Europe/elsewhere opposition that lies behind some of the more modernist definitions of Europeanist ethnology.

The whole idea of an ethnology of the near raises a

double question. In the first place, can an ethnology of Europe lay claim to the same level of sophistication, of conceptual complexity, as the ethnology of remote societies? The answer to this question is generally affirmative, at least on the part of Europeanist ethnologists in a forward-looking context. Thus Martine Segalen, in the collection mentioned above, is able to note with satisfaction that two kinship ethnologists who have worked on the same European region should henceforth be able to talk to one another 'like specialists in the same African ethnic group'; while Anthony P. Cohen points out that kinship studies carried out by Robin Fox on Tory Island and Marilyn Strathern at Elmdon show, on the one hand, the central role of kinship and the strategies based on it in 'our' societies; and, on the other, the plurality of cultures coexisting in a country like present-day Britain.

It must be admitted, though, that in this form the question is baffling. What, one wonders, is being suggested: a possible weakness in the capacity of European societies for symbolization, or the limited ability of Europeanist ethnologists to analyse it?

The second question has an entirely different significance: are the facts, institutions, modes of assembly (work, leisure, residential), modes of circulation specific to the contemporary world, amenable to anthropological scrutiny? For a start, this question does not arise solely – far from it – in relation to

Europe. Anyone with experience of Africa (for example) is well aware that any attempt at an overall anthropological approach must take account of a multitude of interacting elements that arise from immediate reality, but are not readily divisible into 'traditional' and 'modern' categories. It is well known that all the institutional forms that have to be recognized in order to grasp social life (salaried labour, business, spectator sports, the media . . .) play a role, on all the continents, that grows more important by the day. Secondly, it displaces the original question completely: it is not Europe that is under scrutiny but contemporaneity itself, in all the aggressive and disturbing aspects of reality at its most immediate.

It is therefore essential not to confuse the question of method with that of object. It has often been said (not least, on several occasions, by Lévi-Strauss himself) that the modern world lends itself to ethnological observation, however bad we may be at defining areas of observation within reach of our investigative methods. And we know what importance Gérard Althabe (who cannot have realized at the time that he was supplying grist to the mills of our politicians) gave to stairwells, to staircase life, in his studies of big housing estates in Saint-Denis and the Nantes periphery.

It is obvious to anyone who has done fieldwork that ethnological inquiry has limitations which are also assets, and that the ethnologist needs to delineate the approximate limits of a group that he will study, and that will acknowledge him. But there are various aspects. The aspect of method, the need for effective contact with interlocutors, is one thing. The representativeness of the chosen group is another: in effect, it is a matter of being able to assess what the people we see and speak to tell us about the people we do not see and speak to. The field ethnologist's activity throughout is the activity of a social surveyor, a manipulator of scales, a low-level comparative language expert: he cobbles together a significant universe by exploring intermediate universes at need, in rapid surveys; or by consulting relevant documents as a historian. He tries to work out, for himself and others, whom he can claim to be talking about when he talks about the people he has talked to. There is nothing to suggest that the case of some great African kingdom is any different from that of an industrial concern in the Paris suburbs, where this problem of the empirical real object – of representativeness – is concerned.

Two things can be said here, one touching on history and the other on anthropology. Both concern the care that the ethnologist takes to locate the empirical object of his research, to evaluate its qualitative representativeness – for here, strictly speaking, the aim is not to select statistically representative samples but to establish whether what is valid for one lineage, or one village, is valid for others . . . : the difficulty of defining notions like 'tribe' or 'ethnic group' can be seen in this perspective. This concern of ethnologists brings them together with, and at the same time distances them from, historians of microhistory; or – to put it the other way round (for it is ethnologists we are concerned with here) – microhistorians find themselves in the ethnologist's shoes when they are themselves obliged to question the representativeness of the cases they analyse; for example, the life of a fifteenth-century Frioul miller. But in support of this representativeness they have to fall back on notions like 'traces' and 'indications', or resort to exemplary exceptionality; while the field ethnologist, if he is conscientious, can always cast his net a little wider and make sure that what he thought he observed in the first place still holds good. This is the advantage of working on the present, in truth a modest compensation for the essential advantage possessed by all historians: they know what happens afterwards.

The second remark also touches on the object of anthropology, but this time its intellectual object or, if you prefer, the ethnologist's capacity for generalization. It is quite obvious that there is a considerable step between the minute observation of part of a village or the collection of a range of myths from a given population, and the elaboration of a theory on 'elementary kinship structures' or '*mythologiques*'. Structuralism is not the only thing at issue here. All the main anthropological approaches have tended at the very least to generate a range of general hypotheses which may have been inspired initially by examination of a particular case, but have a bearing on the elaboration of problematic configurations going well beyond this case alone: theories of witchcraft, matrimonial alliance, power or relations of production.

Without saying anything here about the validity of these efforts at generalization, we can note their existence as a constituent part of the ethnological literature to point out that the size argument, when it is mentioned in connection with non-exotic societies, concerns only a particular aspect of the research, thus of the method and not the object: neither the empirical object nor, *a fortiori*, the intellectual, theoretical object, which presupposes comparison as well as generalization.

The question of method could not be confused with that of object, for the object of anthropology has never been the exhaustive description of, say, a village or part of a village. When they are produced, monographs of this type are always presented as contributions to a still-incomplete inventory, and usually outline, at least on an empirical level, generalizations more or less based on the research, but applicable to a whole ethnic group. The first question that arises in connection with near-contemporaneity is not whether, or how, it is possible to do fieldwork in a big housing estate, a factory or a holiday camp: that will be managed, either well or badly. The question is whether there are any aspects of contemporary social life that seem to be accessible to anthropological investigation, in the same way that questions of kinship, marriage, bequest, exchange, and so on, came to the attention of anthropologists of the elsewhere, initially as empirical objects, then as objects of reflection (intellectual objects). In this connection, and in the context of the (perfectly legitimate) concerns about method, it is appropriate to refer to what we will call the premiss of the object.

This premiss of the object may raise doubts about the legitimacy of an anthropology of near contemporaneity. Louis Dumont, in his preface to the revised edition of *La Tarasque*, points out (in a passage quoted in Martine Segalen's introduction to *L'Autre et le semblable*) that the 'shifting of centres of interest' and the change of 'problematics' (what we will call here the changes to empirical and intellectual objects) prevent our disciplines from being simply cumulative 'and may even undermine their continuity'. As an example of the shifting of centres of interest he cites in particular, in contrast to the study of popular tradition, a 'way of looking at French social life which is both broader and more finely differentiated, which no longer makes an absolute distinction between the non-modern and the modern, for example between the artisanate and industry'.

I am not convinced that the continuity of a discipline is proportional to that of its objects. The proposition is certainly dubious when it is applied to the life sciences, nor am I sure that these are cumulative in the sense implied by Dumont's phrase: the outcome of research, surely, is new objects of research. It seems to me even more arguable in the case of the social sciences; for when there is change in the modes of grouping and hierarchy it is always social life that is affected, offering the researcher new objects which – like those discovered by the researcher in the life sciences – do not supersede the ones he worked on earlier, but complicate them. That said, however, Louis Dumont's anxiety is not without echoes among those committed to an anthropology of the here and now. An example is the amusing comment in *L'Autre et le semblable* by Gérard Althabe, Jacques Cheyronnaud and Béatrix Le Wita to the effect that the Bretons 'are a lot more worried about their loans from the Crédit Agricole than they are about their genealogies . . .'. Behind this throwaway formulation, the question of the object is outlined once again: why should anthropology attribute more importance to the Bretons' genealogies than they do themselves (although it is hard to imagine Bretons being totally indifferent to them)? If the anthropology of near contemporaneity had to be based exclusively on the categories already registered, if it were not allowed to formulate new objects, then the act of moving into new empirical terrain would not answer a need, merely the researcher's idle curiosity.

★

These premisses call for a positive definition of anthropological research. We will try to formulate one here, starting with two observations.

The first of these concerns anthropological research: anthropological research deals in the present with the question of the other. The question of the other is not just a theme that anthropology encounters from time to time; it is its sole intellectual object, the basis on which different fields of investigation may be defined. It deals with the other in the present; that is sufficient to distinguish it from history. And it deals with it simultaneously in several senses, thus distinguishing itself from the other social sciences.

It deals with all forms of other: the exotic other defined in relation to a supposedly identical 'we' (we French, we Europeans, we Westerners); the other of others, the ethnic or cultural other, defined in relation to a supposedly identical 'they' usually embodied in the name of an ethnic group; the social other, the internal other used as the reference for a system of differences, starting with the division of the sexes but also defining everyone's situation in political, economic and family terms, so that it is not possible to mention a position in the system (elder, younger, next-born, boss, client, captive . . .) without referring to one or more others; and finally the private other – not to be confused with the last – which is present at the heart of all systems of thought and whose (universal) representation is a response to the fact that absolute individuality is unthinkable: heredity, heritage, lineage, resemblance, influence, are all categories through which we may discern an otherness that contributes to, and complements, all individuality. All the literature devoted to the notion of the self, interpretation of sickness and sorcery bears witness to the fact that one of the major questions posed by ethnology is also posed by those it studies: the question concerning what one might call essential or private otherness. Representations of private otherness, in the systems studied by ethnology, place the need for it at the very heart of individuality, at a stroke making it impossible to dissociate the question of collective identity from that of individual identity. This is a remarkable example of what the very content of the beliefs studied by the ethnologist can impose on the approach devised to register it: representation of the individual interests anthropology not just because it is a social construction, but also because any representation of the individual is also a representation of the social link consubstantial with him. By the same token, we are

indebted to the anthropology of remote societies –
and still more to the individuals it studies – for this
discovery: the social begins with the individual; and
the individual is the object of ethnological scrutiny.
The concrete in anthropology is the opposite of the
definition of the concrete accepted by certain schools
of sociological thought: something to be seen in terms
of orders of magnitude from which all individual vari-
ables are eliminated.

Marcel Mauss, discussing the relationship between
psychology and sociology, nevertheless makes a definition of individuality amenable to ethnological
scrutiny which has serious limitations. In a curious
passage, he says in effect that the individual studied by
sociologists is not the man typical of the modern elite,
divided, controlled and conditioned, but the ordinary
or obsolete man who can be defined as a totality:

> The average man today – this is especially true of
> women – along with almost all men in archaic or back-
> ward societies, is a whole; his entire being is affected by
> the smallest of his perceptions or by the slightest mental
> shock. The study of this 'totality' is therefore crucial in
> dealing with all but the elite of our modern societies.
> (Mauss, p. 306)

But the idea of totality – well known to be important
to Mauss, who sees the concrete as the complete –

restricts and, in a sense, mutilates the idea of individuality. More precisely, the individuality he considers is one that represents the culture, a typical individuality. This is confirmed in his analysis of the total social phenomenon, whose interpretation (Lévi-Strauss notes in his 'Introduction to the Work of Marcel Mauss') must include not only all the discontinuous aspects, any one of which (family, technical, economic) could serve as an exclusive basis for the analysis, but also the image that any of its indigenous members has or may have of it. Experience of the total social fact is doubly concrete (and doubly complete): experience of a society precisely located in time and space, but also experience of some individual belonging to that society. But this individual is not just anybody: he is identified with the society of which he is an expression. It is significant that to give an idea of what he means by 'an' individual, Mauss resorts to the definite article: '*the* Melanesian from Island X or Y'. The text quoted above further clarifies this point. The Melanesian is not total only because we perceive him in his different individual dimensions, 'physical, physiological, psychic and sociological', but because his individuality is a synthesis, the expression of a culture which itself is regarded as a whole.

Much could be said (indeed, a fair amount has been said here and there) about this conception of culture and individuality. The fact that in some ways and in some contexts culture and individuality might be defined as reciprocal expressions of one another is a triviality, or anyway a commonplace, which we use when we say, for example, that so-and-so is a 'real' Breton, Briton, Auvergnat or German. The fact that the responses of supposedly free individuals can be assessed or even predicted from those of a statistically significant sample does not surprise us either. It is just that in the meantime we have learned to distrust absolute, simple and substantive identities, on the collective as well as the individual level. Cultures 'work' like green timber, and (for extrinsic and intrinsic reasons) never constitute finished totalities; while individuals, however simple we imagine them to be, are never quite simple enough to become detached from the order that assigns them a position: they express its totality only from a certain angle. Apart from this, the problematic character of all established order would perhaps never manifest itself as such – through wars, revolts, conflicts, tensions – without the triggering flick of an individual initiative. Neither the culture located in time and space, nor the individuals in which it is embodied, defines a base level of identity above which any otherness would become unthinkable. Of course, the culture's 'working' around its fringes, or individual strategies inside its institutional systems, do not always have to be taken into

account in defining (intellectual) research objects.
Discussion and polemic on this point have sometimes
been afflicted by bad faith, or myopia: let us simply
note, for example, that whether or not a rule is
observed – the fact that it might possibly be evaded or
transgressed – has nothing whatever to do with the
examination of all its logical implications, which constitute a genuine research object. But there are other,
different research objects, which do require attention
to be given to procedures of transformation or change,
to gaps, initiatives, transgressions, and so forth.

It is important at least to know what one is talking
about; and it is enough for us here to note that, whatever the level at which anthropological research is
applied, its object is to interpret the interpretation
others make of the category of other on the different
levels that define its place and impose the need for it:
ethnic group, tribe, village, lineage, right down to the
elementary particle of kinship, which is known to
subject the identity of the bloodline to the need for
alliance; and finally the individual, defined by all ritual
systems as a composite steeped in otherness, a figure
who is literally unthinkable (as, in different ways, are
those of the monarch and the sorcerer).

The second observation is not about anthropology
but about the world in which it finds its objects, and
more especially the contemporary world. It is not that
anthropology has become bored with foreign fields

and turned to more familiar terrain, thus risking (as Louis Dumont fears) loss of its continuity; it is that the contemporary world itself, with its accelerated trans-formations, is attracting anthropological scrutiny: in other words, a renewed methodical reflection on the category of otherness. We will examine three of these transformations more closely.

The first is concerned with time, our perception of time but also the use we make of it, the way we dispose of it. For a number of intellectuals, time today is no longer a principle of intelligibility. The idea of progress, which implied an afterwards explainable in terms of what had gone before, has run aground, so to speak, on the shoals of the twentieth century, following the departure of the hopes or illusions that had accompanied the ocean crossing of the nineteenth. To tell the truth, this reassessment refers to several observations that are distinct from one another: the atrocities of the world wars, totalitarianisms and geno-cidal policies, which (to say the very least) do not indicate much moral progress on the part of human-ity; the end of the grand narratives, the great systems of interpretation that aspired to map the evolution of the whole of humanity, but did not succeed, along with the deviation or obliteration of the political sys-tems officially based on some of them; in sum, a doubt as to whether history carries any meaning. Perhaps we should say a renewed doubt, strangely reminiscent of

the one in which Paul Hazard thought he could discern, at the turn of the seventeenth and eighteenth
centuries, the root of the quarrel between the
Ancients and Moderns and the crisis of European
consciousness. But Fontenelle's doubts about history
were focused essentially on its method (anecdotal and
not very reliable), its object (the past speaks to us only
of human folly) and its usefulness (surely young people
really need to know about the period in which they
are going to have to live). When today's historians –
especially in France – have doubts about history, it is
not for technical reasons or reasons concerned with
method (for history has made progress as a science)
but, more fundamentally, because they find it very
difficult to make time into a principle of intelligibility,
let alone a principle of identity.

Moreover, we now see them paying attention to a
number of major themes normally considered
'anthropological' (the family, private life, 'places of
memory'). These researches meet halfway the public's
interest in obsolete forms, which seem to tell our con-
temporaries what they are by showing them what they
are no longer. Nobody expresses this point of view
better than Pierre Nora, in his preface to the first
volume of *Lieux de mémoire*: what we are seeking, he
says in substance, through our religious accumulation
of personal accounts, documents, images and all the
'visible signs of what used to be', is what is different

about us now; and 'within the spectacle of this difference the sudden flash of an unfindable identity. No
longer a genesis, but the deciphering of what we are
in the light of what we are no longer.'

This general finding also corresponds to the decline
of the Sartrean and Marxist references of the early
postwar period, which held that in the final analysis
the universal was the truth of the specific; and to the
rise of what (along with many others) we might call
the postmodern sensibility, the belief that one mode is
worth the same as another, the patchwork of modes
signifying the erasure of modernity as the end product
of an evolution resembling progress.

This theme is inexhaustible, but the question of
time can be looked at from another point of view,
starting with something very commonplace with
which we are confronted every day: the acceleration
of history. We barely have time to reach maturity
before our past has become history, our individual
histories belong to history writ large. People of my
age witnessed in their childhood and adolescence the
tight-lipped nostalgia of men who had fought in the
1914–18 war: it seemed to be telling us that they had
lived through some history (and what history!) but
we would never really be able to understand what it
meant. Nowadays the recent past – 'the sixties', 'the
seventies', now 'the eighties' – becomes history as
soon as it has been lived. History is on our heels,

following us like our shadows, like death. History meaning a series of events recognized as events by large numbers of people (the Beatles, '68, Algeria, Vietnam, Mitterand's victory in '81, Berlin Wall, democratization of East Europe, Gulf War, disintegration of USSR) – events we believe will count in the eyes of future historians and to which each of us, while fully aware that our part in them is as insignificant as Fabrice's at Waterloo, can attach some circumstance or image of a personal, particular nature; as if it were becoming daily less true that men (who else?) make history without knowing it. Surely this very overabundance (in a planet growing smaller by the day – see below) is a problem to the historian of the contemporary?

Let us define this point more precisely. The event or occurrence has always been a problem to those historians who wished to submerge it in the grand sweep of history, who saw it as a pure pleonasm between a before and an after conceived as the development of that before. Behind the polemics, this is the meaning of the analysis of the Revolution (an event if ever there was one) suggested by François Furet. What does he tell us in *Penser la Révolution*? That from the day the Revolution breaks out, the revolutionary event 'institutes a new modality of historic action, one that is not inscribed in the inventory of the situation'. The revolutionary event (and in this sense the

Revolution is exemplary as an event) cannot be reduced to the sum of the factors that make it possible and, after the event, understandable. We would be quite wrong to limit this analysis to the case of the Revolution alone.

The 'acceleration' of history corresponds, in fact, to a multiplication of events very few of which are predicted by economists, historians or sociologists. The problem is the overabundance of events, not the horrors of the twentieth century (whose only new feature – their unprecedented scale – is a by-product of technology), nor its political upheavals and intellectual mutations, of which history offers many other examples. This overabundance, which can be properly appreciated only by bearing in mind both our overabundant information and the growing tangle of interdependences in what some already call the 'world system', causes undeniable difficulties to historians, especially historians of the contemporary – a denomination which the density of events over the last few decades threatens to rob of all meaning. But this problem is precisely anthropological in nature.

Listen to Furet defining the dynamic of the Revolution as an event. It is, he tells us, a dynamic 'that might be called political, ideological or cultural, whose amplified power of mobilizing men and acting on things arises from an overinvestment of meaning' (p. 39). This overinvestment of meaning, exemplarily accessible to anthropological scrutiny, is also apparent in a number of contemporary events (resulting in contradictions whose full scale has yet to be measured); one of these, obviously, is the sudden dissolution of regimes whose fall nobody had dared to predict; but a better example, perhaps, would be the latent crises affecting the political, social and economic life of liberal countries, which we have fallen unconsciously into the habit of discussing in terms of meaning. What is new is not that the world lacks meaning, or has little meaning, or less than it used to have; it is that we seem to feel an explicit and intense daily need to give it meaning: to give meaning to the world, not just some village or lineage. This need to give a meaning to the present, if not the past, is the price we pay for the overabundance of events corresponding to a situation we could call 'supermodern' to express its essential quality: excess.

For each of us has – or thinks he has – the use of it, of this time overloaded with events that encumber the present along with the recent past. This can only – please note – make us even more avid for meaning. The extension of life expectancy, the passage from the normal coexistence of three generations to four, are bringing about gradual, practical changes in the order of social life. By the same token they are expanding the collective, genealogical and historical memory, multiplying the occasions on which an individual can feel his own history intersecting with History, can imagine that the two are somehow connected. The individual's demands and disappointments are linked to the strengthening of this feeling.

So it is with an image of excess – excess of time – that we can start defining the situation of super-modernity, while suggesting that, by the very fact of its contradictions, it offers a magnificent field for observation and, in the full sense of the term, an object of anthropological research. We could say of supermodernity that it is the face of a coin whose obverse represents postmodernity: the positive of a negative. From the viewpoint of supermodernity, the difficulty of thinking about time stems from the over-abundance of events in the contemporary world, not from the collapse of an idea of progress which – at least in the caricatured forms that make its dismissal so very easy – has been in a bad way for a long time; the theme of imminent history, of history snapping at our heels (almost immanent in each of our day-to-day existences) seems like a premiss of the theme of the meaning or non-meaning of history. For it is our need to understand the whole of the present that makes it difficult for us to give meaning to the recent past; the appearance, among individuals in contemporary soci-eties, of a positive demand for meaning (of which the democratic ideal is doubtless an essential aspect) may offer a paradoxical explanation of phenomena which are sometimes interpreted as the signs of a crisis of meaning; for example, the disappointments of all the world's disappointed: disappointment with socialism, with liberalism, and (before long) with post-communism too.

The second accelerated transformation specific to the contemporary world, and the second figure of excess characteristic of supermodernity, concerns space. We could start by saying – again somewhat paradoxically – that the excess of space is correlative with the shrinking of the planet: with the distancing from ourselves embodied in the feats of our astronauts and the endless circling of our satellites. In a sense, our first steps in outer space reduce our own space to an infinitesimal point, of which satellite photographs appropriately give us the exact measure. But at the same time the world is becoming open to us. We are in an era characterized by changes of scale – of course in the context of space exploration, but also on earth: rapid means of transport have brought any capital within a few hours' travel of any other. And in the privacy of our homes, finally, images of all sorts, relayed by satellites and caught by the aerials that bristle on the roofs of our remotest hamlets, can give us an instant, sometimes simultaneous vision of an event taking place on the other side of the planet. Of course we anticipate perverse effects, or possible distortions, from information whose images are selected in this

way: not only can they be (as we say) manipulated, but
the broadcast image (which is only one among count-
less possible others) exercises an influence, possesses a
power far in excess of any objective information it
carries. It should be noted, too, that the screens of the
planet daily carry a mixture of images (news, advertising and fiction) of which neither the presentation nor
the purpose is identical, at least in principle, but which
assemble before our eyes a universe that is relatively
homogeneous in its diversity. What could be more
realistic and, in a sense, more informative about life in
the United States than a good American TV series?
Nor should we forget the sort of false familiarity the
small screen establishes between the viewers and the
actors of big-scale history, whose profiles become as
well known to us as those of soap-opera heroes and
international artistic or sporting stars. They are like the
landscapes in which we regularly watch them playing
out their moves: Texas, California, Washington,
Moscow, the Elysée, Twickenham, the gruelling stages
of the Tour de France or the Arabian desert; we may
not know them personally, but we recognize them.

This spatial overabundance works like a decoy, but
a decoy whose manipulator would be very hard to
identify (there is nobody pulling the strings). In very
large part, it serves as a substitute for the universes
which ethnology has traditionally made its own. We
can say of these universes, which are themselves

broadly fictional, that they are essentially universes of recognition. The property of symbolic universes is that they constitute a means of recognition, rather than knowledge, for those who have inherited them: closed universes where everything is a sign; collections of codes to which only some hold the key but whose existence everyone accepts; totalities which are partially fictional but effective; cosmologies one might think had been invented for the benefit of ethnologists. For this is the point where the ethnologist's fantasies meet those of the indigenous people he studies. One of the major concerns of ethnology has been to delineate signifying spaces in the world, societies identified with cultures conceived as complete wholes: universes of meaning, of which the individuals and groups inside them are just an expression, defining themselves in terms of the same criteria, the same values and the same interpretation procedures.

We will not return to the concepts of culture and individuality criticized above. Suffice it to say that this ideological conception reflects the ethnologists' ideology as much as that of the people they study, and that experience of the supermodern world may help ethnologists to rid themselves of it – or, more precisely, to measure its import. For it rests (among other things) on an organization of space that the space of modernity overwhelms and relativizes. Here too we should make certain things clear: just as the

intelligence of time, it seems to us, is more complicated
by the overabundance of events in the present than
undermined by the radical subversion of prevailing
modes of historical interpretation, so the intelligence
of space is less subverted by current upheavals (for soils
and territories still exist, not just in the reality of facts
on the ground, but even more in that of individual and
collective awareness and imagination) than complicated by the spatial overabundance of the present. This,
as we have seen, is expressed in changes of scale, in the
proliferation of imaged and imaginary references, and
in the spectacular acceleration of means of transport. Its
concrete outcome involves considerable physical
modifications: urban concentrations, movements of
population and the multiplication of what we call
'non-places', in opposition to the sociological notion
of place, associated by Mauss and a whole ethnological
tradition with the idea of a culture localized in time
and space. The installations needed for the accelerated
circulation of passengers and goods (high-speed roads
and railways, interchanges, airports) are just as much
non-places as the means of transport themselves, or
the great commercial centres, or the extended transit
camps where the planet's refugees are parked. For the
time we live in is paradoxical in this aspect, too: at the
very same moment when it becomes possible to think
in terms of the unity of terrestrial space, and the big
multinational networks grow strong, the clamour of

particularisms rises; clamour from those who want to stay at home in peace, clamour from those who want to find a mother country. As if the conservatism of the former and the messianism of the latter were condemned to speak the same language: that of the land and roots.

One might think that the shifting of spatial parameters (spatial overabundance) would confront the ethnologist with difficulties of the same order as those encountered by historians faced with overabundance of events. They may well be of the same order, but where anthropological research is concerned these difficulties are particularly stimulating. Changes of scale, changes of parameter: as in the nineteenth century, we are poised to undertake the study of new civilizations and new cultures.

It matters little that to some extent we may be involved in these as interested parties, for as individuals we are far – very far indeed – from knowing them in all their aspects. Conversely, exotic cultures seemed so different to early Western observers only when they succumbed to the temptation to read them through the ethnocentric grille of their own customary behaviour. Experience of the remote has taught us to de-centre our way of looking, and we should make use of the lesson. The world of supermodernity does not exactly match the one in which we believe we live, for we live in a world that we have not yet learned to look at. We have to relearn to think about space.

The third figure of excess in relation to which the situation of supermodernity might be defined is well known to us. It is the figure of the ego, the individual, who is making a comeback (as they say) in anthropological thought itself, as ethnologists, or some of them, at a loss for new fields in a universe without territories and theoretically breathless in a world without grand narratives, having attempted to deal with cultures (localized cultures, cultures *à la* Mauss) as if they were texts, have reached the point of being interested only in ethnographic description as text; text expressive, naturally, of its author, so that (if we are to believe James Clifford) the Nuer, in the end, teach us more about Evans-Pritchard than he teaches us about them. Without questioning here the spirit of hermeneutic research, whose interpreters construct themselves through the study they make of others, we will suggest that when it is applied to ethnology and ethnological literature, a narrowly based hermeneutics runs the risk of triviality. It is by no means certain that the application of deconstructivist literary criticism to the ethnographic corpus can tell us much that is not banal or obvious (for example, that Evans-Pritchard lived during the colonial era). On the other hand, it is quite possible that ethnology will be straying from the true path if it replaces its fields of study with the study of those who have done fieldwork.

But postmodern anthropology (to give the devil his due) does seem to depend on an analysis of super-modernity, of which its reductivist method (field to text, text to author) is in fact just a particular expression.

In Western societies, at least, the individual wants to be a world in himself; he intends to interpret the information delivered to him by himself and for himself. Sociologists of religion have revealed the singular character even of Catholic practice: practising Catholics intend to practise in their own fashion. Similarly, the question of relations between the sexes can be settled only in the name of the undifferentiated value of the individual. Note, though, that this individualization of approaches seems less surprising when it is referred to the analyses outlined above: never before have individual histories been so explicitly affected by collective history, but never before, either, have the reference points for collective identification been so unstable. The individual production of meaning is thus more necessary than ever. Naturally, sociology is perfectly placed to expose the illusions on which this individualization of approaches is based, and the effects of reproduction and stereotyping which wholly or partly escape the notice of the players. But the singular character of the production of meaning, backed by a whole advertising apparatus (which talks of the body, the senses, the freshness of living) and a whole political language (hinged on the theme of individual freedoms), is interesting in itself. It relates to what ethnologists have studied among foreigners under various headings: what might be called local anthropologies (rather than cosmologies), the systems of representation in which the categories of identity and otherness are given shape.

So anthropologists are today facing, in new terms, a problem that raises the same difficulties that Mauss, and after him the culturalist school, confronted in their day: how to think about and situate the individual. Michel de Certeau, in *L'Invention du quotidien*, talks about 'tricks in the arts of doing' that enable individuals subjected to the global constraints of modern – especially urban – society to deflect them, to make use of them, to contrive through a sort of everyday tinkering to establish their own decor and trace their own personal itineraries. But, as Michel de Certeau was aware, these tricks and these arts of doing refer sometimes to the multiplicity of average individuals (the ultimate in concreteness), sometimes to the average of individuals (an abstraction). Similarly Freud, in his 'sociological' works *Civilization and its Discontents* and *The Future of an Illusion*, uses the expression 'ordinary man' – *der gemeine Mann* – to contrast, rather as Mauss does, the general run of indi-

viduals with the enlightened elite: those human individuals capable of making themselves the object of a
reflective approach.

Freud is perfectly well aware, however, that the
alienated man of whom he writes – alienated from
various institutions: religion for example – is also all
mankind or Everyman, starting with Freud himself or
anyone else in a position to observe at first hand the
mechanisms and effects of alienation. This necessary
alienation is clearly the one Lévi-Strauss means when
he writes in his 'Introduction to the Work of Marcel
Mauss' that, strictly speaking, it is the person we consider healthy in mind who is alienated, since he agrees
to exist in a world defined by relations with others.

Freud, as we know, practised self-analysis. The
question facing anthropologists today is how best to
integrate the subjectivity of those they observe into
their analysis: in other words, how to redefine the
conditions of representativeness to take account of the
renewed status of the individual in our societies. We
cannot rule out the possibility that the anthropologist,
following Freud's example, might care to consider
himself as indigenous to his own culture – a privileged
informant, so to speak – and risk a few attempts at
ethno-self-analysis.

Beyond the heavy emphasis placed today on the
individual reference (or, if you prefer, the individualization of references), attention should really be given

to factors of singularity: singularity of objects, of groups or memberships, the reconstruction of places; the singularities of all sorts that constitute a paradoxical counterpoint to the procedures of interrelation, acceleration and de-localization sometimes carelessly reduced and summarized in expressions like 'homogenization of culture' or 'world culture'.

The question of the conditions for practising an anthropology of contemporaneity should be transferred from the method to the object. This is not to suggest that questions of method do not have decisive importance, or that they can be entirely dissociated from the question of object. But the question of object comes first. It can even be said to constitute a double premiss, because before taking an interest in the new social forms, modes of sensibility or institutions that may seem characteristic of present contemporaneity we need to pay some attention to the changes affecting the major categories people use when they think about their identity and their reciprocal relations. The three figures of excess which we have employed to characterize the situation of supermodernity – overabundance of events, spatial overabundance, the individualization of references – make it possible to grasp the idea of supermodernity without ignoring its complexities and contradictions, but also without treating it as the uncrossable horizon of a lost modernity with which nothing remains to be done except to map its traces, list its isolates and index its files. The twenty-first century will be anthropological, not only because the three figures of excess are just the current form of a perennial raw material which is the very ore of anthropology, but also because in situations of supermodernity (as in the situations anthropology has analysed under the name of 'acculturation') the components pile up without destroying one another. So we can reassure in advance those passionately devoted to the phenomena studied by anthropology (from marriage to religion, from exchange to power, from possession to witchcraft): they are not about to disappear from Africa, or from Europe either. But they will make sense again (they will remake meaning), along with all the rest, in a different world, whose reasons and unreasons the anthropologists of tomorrow, just like those of today, will have to try to understand.

Anthropological Place

The place held in common by the ethnologist and those he talks about is simply a place: the one occupied by the indigenous inhabitants who live in it, cultivate it, defend it, mark its strong points and keep its frontiers under surveillance, but who also detect in it the traces of chthonian or celestial powers, ancestors or spirits which populate and animate its private geography; as if the small fragment of humanity making them offerings and sacrifices in this place were also the quintessence of humanity, as if there were no humanity worthy of the name except in the very place of the cult devoted to them.

The ethnologist, on the contrary, sets out to decipher, from the way the place is organized (the frontier always postulated and marked out between wild nature and cultivated nature, the permanent or temporary allotment of cultivable land or fishing grounds, the layout of villages, the arrangement of housing and rules of residence – in short, the group's economic, social, political and religious geography), an order which is all the more restrictive – in any case, the more obvious – because its transcription in space gives it the appearance of a second nature. The ethnologist thus sees himself as the most subtle and knowledgeable of the inhabitants.

This place common to the ethnologist and its indigenous inhabitants is in one sense (the sense of the Latin word *invenire*) an invention: it has been discovered by those who claim it as their own. Foundation narratives are only rarely narratives about autochthony; more often they are narratives that bring the spirits of the place together with the first inhabitants in the common adventure of the group in movement. The social demarcation of the soil is the more necessary for not always being original. For his part, the ethnologist examines this demarcation. It may even happen that his intervention and curiosity restore to those among whom he is working an interest in their own origins which may have been attenuated, even completely stifled, by phenomena connected with more recent actuality: urban migrations, the arrival of new populations, the spread of industrial cultures.

A reality certainly lies at the origin of this double invention, and provides its raw material and its object. But it may also give rise to fantasies and illusions: the indigenous fantasy of a society anchored since time immemorial in the permanence of an intact soil outside which nothing is really understandable; the ethnologist's illusion of a society so transparent to itself that it is fully expressed in the most trivial of its usages, in any one of its institutions, and in the total personality of each of its members. Knowledge of the systematic mapping of nature carried out by all societies, even nomadic ones, extends the fantasy and feeds the illusion.

The indigenous fantasy is that of a closed world founded once and for all long ago; one which, strictly speaking, does not have to be understood. Everything there is to know about it is already known: land, forest, springs, notable features, religious places, medicinal plants, not forgetting the temporal dimensions of an inventory of these places whose legitimacy is postulated, and whose stability is supposed to be assured, by narratives about origins and by the ritual calendar. All the inhabitants have to do is *recognize* themselves in it when the occasion arises. Every unexpected event, even one that is wholly predictable and recurrent from the ritual point of view (like birth, illness or death), demands to be interpreted not, really, in order to be known, but in order to be recognized:

to be made accessible to a discourse, a diagnosis, in terms that are already established, whose announcement will not be liable to shock the guardians of cultural orthodoxy and social syntax. It is hardly surprising that the terms of this discourse should tend to be spatial, once it has become clear that it is the spatial arrangements that express the group's identity (its actual origins are often diverse, but the group is established, assembled and united by the identity of the place), and that the group has to defend against external and internal threats to ensure that the language of identity retains a meaning.

One of my first ethnological experiences, the interrogation of a cadaver in Alladian country, was exemplary from this point of view; all the more exemplary since, with variable details, the practice is very widespread in West Africa, and equivalent techniques are found in other parts of the world. Basically it involved making the cadaver say whether the person responsible for his death was to be found outside the Alladian villages or in one of them; in the village where the ceremony took place or outside it (and in this case, whether to east or west); inside or outside his own lineage, his own house, and so on. It might sometimes happen that the cadaver would short-circuit the slow progress of the interrogation, pulling his troop of bearers towards a compound and smashing down the palisade or front door, thus indicating to his questioners that they need look no further. We can hardly do better than to say that the identity of the ethnic group (in this case the composite group the Alladian happen to be), which obviously presupposes a thorough mastery of its internal tensions, is maintained through a constant re-examination of the condition of its external and internal frontiers which, significantly, have (or had) to be restated, repeated, reaffirmed on the occasion of almost every individual death.

The fantasy of a founded, ceaselessly re-founding place is only half fantasy. For a start, it works well – or rather, it has worked well: land has been cultivated, nature domesticated, reproduction of the generations ensured; in this sense the gods of the soil have looked after it well. The territory has been maintained against external aggressions and internal splits, something we know is not always the case: in this sense, too, the apparatuses for divination and prevention have been effective. This effectiveness can be measured on the scale of the family, the lineage, the village or the group. Those who take responsibility for coping with sudden vicissitudes, who uncover and resolve particular difficulties, are always more numerous than those who fall victim to or are threatened by them: everyone holds fast and everything stays together.

It is also a semi-fantasy because, although nobody doubts the reality of the place held in common and the powers that threaten it or protect it, nobody is unaware – nobody has ever been unaware – of the reality of other groups (in Africa, many foundation narratives are basically narratives of war and flight) and thus also of other gods; or of the need to trade and marry outside. There is nothing to suggest that, yesterday or today, the image of a closed and self-sufficient world could ever – even to those who diffuse it and therefore identify with it – be anything other than a useful and necessary image: not a lie but a myth, roughly inscribed on the soil, fragile as the territory whose singularity it founds, subject (as frontiers are) to possible readjustment, and for this very reason doomed always to regard the most recent migration as the first foundation.

It is at this point that the indigenous population's semi-fantasy converges with the ethnologist's illusion. This, too, is only a semi-illusion. For although the ethnologist can hardly help being tempted to identify the people he studies with the landscape in which he finds them, the space they have shaped, he is just as aware as they are of the vicissitudes of their history, their mobility, the multiplicity of spaces to which they refer, the fluctuation of their frontiers. Moreover, he may be tempted, like them, to look back from the upheavals of the present towards an illusory past stability. When bulldozers deface the landscape, the young people run off to the city or 'allochthones' move in, it is in the most concrete, the most spatial sense that the landmarks – not just of the territory, but of identity itself – are erased.

But this is not the crucial part of the ethnologist's temptation, which is intellectual and has long been a feature of the ethnological tradition.

Calling on a notion that this tradition has itself used and abused under various circumstances, we will name this the 'totality temptation'. Let us return for a moment to Mauss's use of the notion of total social fact and Lévi-Strauss's commentary on it. The totality of the social fact, according to Mauss, refers back to two other totalities: the sum of different institutions that go into its make-up, but also the whole range of different dimensions that serve to define the individuality of all those who live in it and take part in it. As we have seen, Lévi-Strauss summarizes this point of view in remarkable fashion by suggesting that the total social fact is primarily the social fact perceived totally: in other words, an interpretation of the social fact which includes the picture any of its indigenous members might have of it. But this ideal of exhaustive interpretation, which a novelist would find discouraging owing to the comprehensive imaginative effort it might seem to require of him, rests on a very particular conception of the 'average' man, in which he too is defined as 'total' because, unlike the representatives of the modern elite, 'his entire being is affected by the smallest of his perceptions or by the slightest mental shock' (p. 306). For Mauss, the 'average' man in modern society is anyone who does not belong to the elite. But archaism knows nothing but the average. The 'average' man resembles 'almost all men in archaic or backward societies' in the sense that, like them, he displays a vulnerability and permeability to his immediate surroundings that specifically enable him to be defined as 'total'.

Nevertheless, it is not at all certain that Mauss regards modern society as an amenable ethnological object; because the ethnologist's object, to him, is a society precisely located in space and time. In the ethnologist's ideal territory (that of archaic or 'backward' societies), all men are 'average' (we could say 'representative'); location in time and space is therefore easy to achieve there: it applies to everyone, and elements like class divisions, migration, urbanization and industrialization do not intrude to scale down its dimensions and make it more difficult to read. Behind the ideas of totality and localized society there clearly lies another: that of consistency or transparency between culture, society and individual.

The idea of culture as text, which is one of the more recent manifestations of American culturalism, is already present in its entirety in the notion of localized society. When Mauss illustrates the need to integrate into the analysis of the total social fact the view of 'any individual' belonging to the society by referring to 'the Melanesian from Island X or Y', it is significant, certainly, that he resorts to use of the definite article (this Melanesian is a prototype, like many another ethnic subject promoted to exemplarity at other times and under other skies), but also that an island – a small island – should be offered as an example of the ideal setting for a cultural totality. The contours and frontiers of an island can be designated or traced without difficulty; and within an archipelago, from island to island, circuits of navigation and exchange form fixed and recognized itineraries that draw a clear frontier between the zone of relative identity (recognized identity and established relations) and the external world, a world of absolute foreignness. The ideal, for an ethnologist wishing to characterize singular particularities, would be for each ethnic group to have its own island, possibly linked to others but different from any other; and for each islander to be an exact replica of his neighbours.

In so far as the culturalist view of societies tries to be systematic, its limitations are obvious: to substantify a singular culture is to ignore its intrinsically problematic character (sometimes brought to light, however, by its reactions to other cultures or to the jolts of history); to ignore, too, a complexity of social tissue and a variety of individual positions which could never be deduced from the cultural 'text'. But it

would be wrong to overlook the element of reality
that underlies the indigenous fantasy and the ethnological illusion: the organization of space and the
founding of places, inside a given social group,
comprise one of the stakes and one of the modalities
of collective and individual practice. Collectivities (or
those who direct them), like their individual members, need to think simultaneously about identity and
relations; and to this end, they need to symbolize the
components of shared identity (shared by the whole of
a group), particular identity (of a given group or individual in relation to others) and singular identity (what
makes the individual or group of individuals different
from any other). The handling of space is one of the
means to this end, and it is hardly astonishing that the
ethnologist should be tempted to follow in reverse
the route from space to the social, as if the latter had
produced the former once and for all. This route is
essentially 'cultural' since, when it passes through the
most visible, the most institutionalized signs, those
most recognized by the social order, it simultaneously
designates the place of the social order, defined by the
same stroke as a common place.

We will reserve the term 'anthropological place'
for this concrete and symbolic construction of space,
which could not of itself allow for the vicissitudes and
contradictions of social life, but which serves as a reference for all those it assigns to a position, however

humble and modest. Moreover, it is because all anthropology is anthropology of other people's anthropology that place – anthropological place – is a principle of meaning for the people who live in it, and also a principle of intelligibility for the person who observes it. Anthropological place functions on a variable scale. The Kabyle house with its shade side and its light side, its masculine part and feminine part; the Mina or Ewe house with its internal *legba* to protect the sleeper from his own drives and its threshold *legba* to protect him from outside aggression; the dualist layouts, often embodied on the ground in a highly material and visible frontier, which directly or indirectly order alliance, exchange, games and religion; Ebrié or Atyé villages, whose three-way division orders the life of the clans and age-classes: all are places whose analysis has meaning because they have been invested with meaning, the need for which is endorsed and confirmed by every new circuit and every ritual reiteration.

These places have at least three characteristics in common. They want to be – people want them to be – places of identity, of relations and of history. The layout of the house, the rules of residence, the zoning of the village, placement of altars, configuration of public open spaces, land distribution, correspond for every individual to a system of possibilities, prescriptions and interdicts whose content is both spatial and social. To be born is to be born in a place, to be 'assigned to residence'.[2] In this sense the actual place of birth is a constituent of individual identity. It often happens in Africa that a child who is born by chance outside the village receives a particular name derived from some feature of the landscape in which the birth took place. The birthplace obeys the law of the 'proper' (and of the proper name) mentioned by Michel de Certeau.

Louis Marin, for his part, borrows Furetière's Aristotelian definition of place ('Primary and immobile surface of a body which surrounds another body or, to speak more clearly, the space in which a body is placed'[3]) and quotes his example: 'Every body occupies its place.' But this singular and exclusive occupation is more that of a cadaver in its grave than of the nascent or living body. In the order of birth and life the proper place, like absolute individuality, becomes more difficult to define and think about. Michel de Certeau perceives the place, of whatever sort, as containing the order 'in whose terms elements are distributed in relations of coexistence' and,

---

2. This expression is used in French to mean 'placed under house arrest'. [Tr.]

3. Louis Marin, 'Le lieu du pouvoir à Versailles', in *La Production des lieux exemplaires*, Les Dossiers des séminaires TTS, 1991, p. 89.

although he rules out the possibility of two things occupying the same 'spot', although he admits that every element of the place adjoins others, in a specific 'location', he defines the 'place' as an 'instantaneous configuration of positions' (p. 173), which boils down to saying that the elements coexisting in the same place may be distinct and singular, but that does not prevent us from thinking either about their interrelations, or about the shared identity conferred on them by their common occupancy of the place. Thus, the rules of residence which assign the child to his position (usually with his mother, and therefore also with his father, his maternal uncle or his maternal grandmother) situate him in an overall configuration whose inscription on the soil he shares with others.

Finally, place becomes necessarily historical from the moment when – combining identity with relations – it is defined by a minimal stability. This is the case even though those who live in it may recognize landmarks there which do not have to be objects of knowledge. Anthropological place is historical, for them, to the precise extent that it escapes history as science. This place which the ancestors have built ('More pleasing to me is the abode my forefathers have built . . .'[4]), which the recently dead populate

---

4. Joachim du Bellay (1522–60), poet, friend and collaborator of Ronsard. [Tr.]

with signs whose evocation and interpretation require special knowledge, whose tutelary powers are awakened and reactivated at regular intervals dictated by a precise ritual timetable: this is the antithesis of the 'places of memory' of which Pierre Nora so aptly writes that what we see in them is essentially how we have changed, the image of what we are no longer. The inhabitant of an anthropological place does not make history; he lives in it. The difference between these two relationships to history is still very clear to my generation of Frenchmen and women, who lived through the 1940s and were able in the village (perhaps only a place they visited for holidays) to attend Corpus Christi, Rogation days or the annual feast-day of some local patron saint ordinarily tucked away in an isolated chapel: when these processions and observances disappear, their memory does not simply remind us, like other childhood memories, of the passage of time or the changing individual; they have effectively disappeared – or rather, they have been transformed: the feast is still celebrated from time to time, to do things the old way, just as a little threshing is done in the old way every summer; the chapel has been restored and a concert or show is sometimes put on there. These refurbishments cause a few perplexed smiles and a certain amount of retrospective musing among the older locals: for what they see projected at a distance is the place where they used to believe they lived from day to day, but which they are now being invited to see as a fragment of history. Spectators of themselves, tourists of the private, they can hardly be expected to blame nostalgia or tricks of memory for objectively evident changes to the space in which they still live, which is no longer the place where they used to live.

Of course, the intellectual status of anthropological place is ambiguous. It is only the idea, partially materialized, that the inhabitants have of their relations with the territory, with their families and with others. This idea may be partial or mythologized. It varies with the individual's point of view and position in society. Nevertheless, it offers and imposes a set of references which may not be quite those of natural harmony or some 'paradise lost', but whose absence, when they disappear, is not easily filled. The ethnologist, for his part, is especially responsive to everything written on the soil, in the life of those he observes, which signifies closure, careful control of relations with the outside, the immanence of the divine in the human, or the close connection between the necessity for a sign and its meaning. He is sensitive to these things because he carries their image, and the need for them, within himself.

If we linger for a moment on the definition of anthropological place we will see, first, that it is geometric. It can be mapped in terms of three simple spatial forms, which apply to different institutional arrangements and in a sense are the elementary forms of social space. In geometric terms these are the line, the intersection of lines, and the point of intersection. Concretely, in the everyday geography more familiar to us, they correspond to routes, axes or paths that lead from one place to another and have been traced by people; to crossroads and open spaces where people pass, meet and gather, and which sometimes (in the case of marketplaces, for example) are made very large to satisfy the needs of economic exchange; and lastly, to centres of more or less monumental type, religious or political, constructed by certain men and therefore defining a space and frontiers beyond which other men are defined as others, in relation with other centres and other spaces.

But routes, crossroads and centres are not absolutely independent notions. There is a partial overlap. A route may pass through different points of interest, all of which may be places of assembly; sometimes markets define fixed points on a route; and although the market itself may be the centre of attraction, the space where it is held may also contain a monument (the shrine of a god, the palace of a sovereign) marking the centre of a different social space. This combination of spaces corresponds to a certain institutional complexity. Big markets require specific forms of political control; they exist only by virtue of a contract, respect for which is ensured by various religious or political procedures: for example, they are places of sanctuary. As for routes, they cross an assortment of frontiers and limits which are obviously not intrinsic or self-evident, and are therefore known to need special economic or ritual arrangements to make them work.

These simple forms are not characteristic only of great political or economic spaces; they also define village space or domestic space. In his book *Mythe et pensée chez les Grecs*, Jean-Pierre Vernant shows how, in the Hestia/Hermes couple, Hestia symbolizes the circular hearth placed in the centre of the house, the closed space of the group withdrawn into itself (and thus in a sense of its relations with itself); while Hermes, god of the threshold and the door, but also of crossroads and town gates, represents movement and relations with others. Identity and relations lie at the heart of all the spatial arrangements classically studied by anthropology.

So does history. For all relations that are inscribed in space are also inscribed in time, and the simple spatial forms we have mentioned are concretized only in and through time. First of all, their reality is historical: in Africa (and elsewhere) the foundation narratives of villages or kingdoms often trace a whole journey, punctuated by various preliminary stops, before the final, definitive establishment. We know too that markets (like political capitals) have histories; that some are created as others fade away. A date can be put on the acquisition or creation of a god, and the same applies to cults and sanctuaries as to markets and political capitals: whether they endure or not, whether they are expanding or shrinking, the space in which they grow or regress is a historical space.

We ought to say a few words on the materially temporal dimension of these spaces. Itineraries are measured in hours or days of travel. The marketplace merits its title only on certain days. In West Africa it is easy to identify zones of exchange within which there is a weekly rotation of market days and marketplaces. Places devoted to cults, to political or religious assembly, fulfil this role only at certain moments, generally on fixed dates. Initiation ceremonies and fertility rituals take place at regular intervals: the religious or social calendar is ordinarily modelled on the agricultural calendar, and the sacral quality of the places in which ritual activity is concentrated might be described as an alternating sacrality. This, incidentally, is what creates the conditions for the memory attached to certain places, which helps to underline their sacred character. According to Durkheim, in *Les Formes élémentaires de la vie religieuse*, the notion of the sacred is linked to the retrospective element stemming from the alternating character of the feast or ceremony. When he sees the Jewish Passover and a veterans' reunion as equally 'religious' or 'sacred', it is because they give the participants the opportunity not only to remind themselves of the group to which they belong, but also to remember earlier celebrations.

The monument, as the Latin etymology of the word indicates, is an attempt at the tangible expression of permanence or, at the very least, duration. Gods need shrines, as sovereigns need thrones and palaces, to place them above temporal contingencies. They thus enable people to think in terms of continuity through the generations. This is well expressed, in a way, by one of the interpretations of traditional African nosology: that an illness can be imputed to the action of a god angered by the way his shrine is neglected by its builder's successor. Without the monumental illusion before the eyes of the living, history would be a mere abstraction. The social space bristles with monuments – imposing stone buildings, discreet mud shrines – which may not be directly functional but give every individual the justified feeling that, for the most part, they pre-existed him and will survive him. Strangely, it is a set of breaks and discontinuities in space that expresses continuity in time.

This magical effect of spatial construction can be attributed without hesitation to the fact that the human body itself is perceived as a portion of space with frontiers and vital centres, defences and weaknesses, armour and defects. At least on the level of the imagination (entangled in many cultures with that of

social symbolism), the body is a composite and hierarchized space which can be invaded from the outside.
Examples do exist of territories conceived in the
image of the human body, but the inverse – the
human body conceived as a territory – is very widespread. In West Africa, for example, the components
of the personality are conceived in terms of a topography recalling the Freudian topography, but applied
to realities conceived as being substantially material.
Thus in the Akan civilizations (of present-day Ghana
and the Ivory Coast) the psyche of each individual is
defined by two 'entities'; the material character of
their existence is indicated directly by the fact that
one of them is assimilated to the shadow cast by the
body, and indirectly by the fact that weakness of the
body is attributed to the weakness or departure of one
of them. Health is defined by their perfect coinci-
dence. On the other hand, a person may be killed if
awakened suddenly, as one of these 'entities', the double that wanders by night, may not have time to
reoccupy the body at the moment of waking.

The internal organs themselves or certain parts of
the body (kidneys, head, big toe) are often conceived
as autonomous, sometimes the abode of an ancestral
presence and for this reason the object of specific
cults. In this way the body becomes a collection of
religious places; zones are set aside as objects
for anointment or purification. Here the effects

mentioned above in connection with the construction of space are seen in play on the human body itself. Dream journeys become dangerous when they venture too far from the body conceived as a centre. This centred body is also the site of the convergence or meeting of ancestral elements, a meeting possessing monumental value because it involves elements that existed before the ephemeral carnal envelope, and will survive it. Sometimes the mummification of a body or the erection of a tomb completes the transformation of the body into a monument after death.

Thus, starting from simple spatial forms, we see how the individual thematic and the collective thematic intersect and combine. Political symbolism plays on these possibilities to express the power of an authority, employing the unity of a sovereign figure to unify and symbolize the internal diversities of a social collectivity. Sometimes this is done by distinguishing the king's body from other bodies as a multiple body. The theme of the king's double body is wholly pertinent in Africa. Thus the Agni king of the Sanwi, in the present-day Ivory Coast, had a double, a slave by origin, who was called Ekala (after one of the two components or entities mentioned above): with two bodies and two *ekala* – his own and that of his slave double – the Agni sovereign was thought to have particularly effective protection, the body of the slave double obstructing any aggression aimed at the king's person. If he failed in this role and the king died, the *ekala* would naturally follow him into the grave. More remarkable, however, and more widely attested than multiplication of the king's body, are the concentration and condensation of the space in which sovereign authority is localized. The sovereign is very frequently under a sort of house arrest, condemned to semi-immobility, to hours of exposure on the royal throne, presented as an object to his subjects. Frazer – and, through him, Durkheim – was struck by this passivity/massivity of the sovereign body, and noticed that it was a feature common to monarchies very remote from one another in time and space – for example, ancient Mexico, Africa around the Bight of Benin, and Japan. Especially remarkable in all these examples is the possibility that an object (throne, crown), or another human body, might sometimes be considered an acceptable substitute for the sovereign's body in fulfilling the function of fixed centre of the kingdom, which involves spending long hours in a state of mineral immobility.

This immobility, and the narrowness of the confines containing the sovereign figure, quite literally form a centre that underlines the permanence of the dynasty, and orders and unifies the internal diversity of the social body. Note that the identification of power with the place where it is exercised, or the monument that houses its representatives, has become a constant of political discourse in modern states. Anyone naming the White House or the Kremlin is referring simultaneously to a monumental place, a human individual, and a power structure. Successive metonymies have given us the habit of designating a country by its capital and a capital by the name of the building occupied by its rulers. Political language is naturally spatial (if only in its use of the concepts left and right), doubtless because of its need to think simultaneously about unity and diversity; and centrality is the most approximate, the most imaged and the most material expression of this double and contradictory intellectual constraint.

The notions of itinerary, intersection, centre and monument are useful not only for the description of traditional anthropological places. They can also be applied to contemporary French space, urban space in particular. Paradoxically, they even enable us to characterize it as a specific space although, by definition, they are criteria of comparison.

It is usual to describe France as a centralized country. It certainly is one on the political level, at least since the seventeenth century; and despite recent efforts at regionalization, it is still a centralized country on the administrative level (the initial ideal of the French Revolution had even been to divide up the administrative constituencies along rigidly geometric lines). It remains one in the minds of the French, as a result notably of the layout of its road and rail networks, both conceived, at least initially, as spiders' webs with Paris at the centre.

To be more precise, not only is Paris laid out more like a capital than any other in the world, but there is not a town in France that does not aspire to be the centre of a region of variable size, or has not managed over the years and centuries to build itself a monumental centre (what we call the 'town centre') to symbolize and materialize this aspiration. The smallest French towns, even villages, always boast a 'town centre' containing monuments that symbolize religious authority (church or cathedral) and civil authority (town hall, *sous-préfecture* or, in big towns, the *préfecture*). The church (Catholic in most parts of France) overlooks a square or open space through which many or most cross-town routes pass. The town hall is nearby; even where this defines a space of its own, the place de la Mairie is seldom more than a stone's throw from the place de l'Eglise. Also in the town centre, and always close to the town hall and the church, a monument to the dead has been erected. Lay in concept, this is not really a religious place but a monument whose value is historical (a memorial to the dead of two world wars whose names are graven in the stone): on certain annual feast-days, notably the 11th of November, the civil and sometimes military authorities commemorate there the sacrifice of those who have fallen for their country. These so-called 'commemoration services' correspond fairly closely to the enlarged – in other words, social – definition Durkheim suggests for the religious phenomenon. Doubtless they derive a particular efficacy from happening in a place where the intimacy between the living and the dead was once expressed in more everyday fashion: in many villages we still find the trace of a layout going back to medieval times, when the church, surrounded by the cemetery, lay at the very centre of active social life.

The town centre is an active place. Under the traditional conception of provincial towns and villages (brought to literary life during the first half of this century by authors like Giraudoux and Jules Romain), in towns and villages as they appeared under the Third Republic and to a large extent still appear today, the leading cafés, hotels and businesses are concentrated in the town centre, not far from the square where the market is held (when, that is, market square and church square are not one and the same). At regular weekly intervals, on Sunday or Market Day, the centre 'comes to life'. The new towns produced by technicist and voluntarist urbanization projects have often been criticized for failing to offer 'places for living', equivalent to those produced by an older, slower history: where individual itineraries can intersect and mingle, where a few words are exchanged and solitudes momentarily forgotten, on the church steps, in front of the town hall, at the café counter or in the baker's doorway: the rather lazy rhythm and talkative mood that still characterize Sunday mornings in contemporary provincial France.

This France could be defined as a whole, a cluster of centres of greater or lesser importance that polarize the administrative, festive and trading activities of a region of variable size. The organization of routes – the road system linking these centres to each other through a network, actually very close-grained, of trunk roads (between centres of national importance) and departmental roads (between centres of departmental importance) – is wholly in keeping with this polycentred and hierarchized layout: on the kilometre stones which punctuate roads at regular intervals, the distance to the nearest settlement used to be inscribed along with the distance to the nearest large town. Today this information tends to appear more legibly on big signs appropriate to the intensified and accelerated traffic.

Every settlement in France aspires to be the centre of a significant space and of at least one specific activity. Thus Lyon, a large metropolis, claims among other titles that of 'capital of gastronomy'; the small town of Thiers can call itself the 'cutlery capital'; Digouin, a big market town, is the 'pottery capital'; and Janzé, really no more than a large village, boasts that it is the

'birthplace of the free-range chicken'. These claims to
various forms of glory appear today at the settlements'
boundaries, along with signs mentioning their twin-
ning with towns or villages elsewhere in Europe. In a
way, these signs give proof of modernity and integra-
tion in the new European economic space. They
coexist with other signs (and information boards) giving a detailed account of the historic curiosities of the
place: fourteenth- or fifteenth-century chapels, castles
and palaces, megaliths, museums of crafts, lace or pottery. Historical depth is vaunted in the same breath as
openness to the outside world, as if the one were
equivalent to the other. Every town or village not of
recent origin lays public claim to its history, displaying
it to the passing motorist on a series of signboards
which add up to a sort of 'business card'. Making the
historical context explicit in this way, which in fact is
quite a recent practice, coincides with a reorganization
of space (the creation of bypasses and main motorway
routes avoiding towns) that tends, inversely, to short-
circuit the historical context by avoiding the
monuments that embody it. It may be interpreted
quite legitimately as an attempt to attract and hold the
attention of the passer-by, the tourist; but it can have
some measure of effectiveness only in combination
with the taste for history, for identities rooted in the
soil, which has become an undeniable feature of
French sensibility over the past twenty years. The

dated monument is cited as a proof of authenticity which ought in itself to arouse interest: a gap is opened up between the landscape's present and the past to which it alludes. The allusion to the past complicates the present.

We might add that a minimal historical dimension has always been imparted to French urban and village space by the choice of street names. Streets and squares have always been used for commemoration. Of course it is traditional for certain monuments – with an effect of redundancy which, incidentally, is not without charm – to lend their names to the streets leading up to them, or the squares on which they are built. Thus we long ago lost count of rues de la Gare, rues du Théâtre and places de la Mairie. But the main streets in towns and villages are more usually named after notables of local or national life, or great events of national history; so that to write an exegesis of all the street names in a metropolis like Paris one would have to review the entire history of France, from Vercingetorix to de Gaulle. Anyone who regularly takes the Metro, who learns the Paris Underground and its station names echoing the streets or monuments on the surface, experiences a sort of mechanized daily immersion in history that conditions Parisians to think of Alésia, Bastille and Solférino as spatial landmarks rather than historical references.

Roads and crossroads in France thus tend to

become 'monuments' (in the sense of testimonies and reminders) when the names they have been given immerse them in history. These incessant references to history cause frequent cross-connections between the notions of itineraries, crossroads and monuments. The connections are particularly clear in towns (especially Paris), where historical references are always more densely encrusted. Paris does not have one centre; on motorway signs, central Paris is indicated sometimes by the image of the Eiffel Tower, sometimes by the formula 'Paris–Notre-Dame', which refers to the original historic heart of the capital, the Île de la Cité, encirled by the river Seine a few kilometres from the Eiffel Tower. So there are several centres in Paris. On the administrative level, we should note an ambiguity which has always caused problems in our political life (showing clearly how centralized this is): Paris is both a town, divided into twenty *arrondissements*, and the capital of France. On a number of occasions the Parisians have believed themselves to be making the history of France, a conviction (rooted in memories of 1789) which has been known to cause tension between the national government and the municipal government. Until very recently, apart from a short period during the revolution of 1848, Paris has done without a mayor since 1795; the capital's twenty *arrondissements* have been run by their twenty town halls under the joint supervision of the prefect of the department of la Seine and the prefect of police. The municipal council dates only from 1834. When the statutes of the capital were reformed a few years ago and Jacques Chirac became mayor of Paris, part of the political debate was about whether or not this post would help him become President of the Republic. Nobody really thought he would want to run a town – even one containing a sixth of the French population – as an end in itself. The existence of three Parisian palaces (the Elysée, Matignon and the Hôtel de Ville), whose vocations are distinct (albeit with a very problematic distinctness), plus at least two other monuments of equivalent importance, the Palais du Luxembourg (seat of the Senate) and the National Assembly (where the deputies sit), shows pretty clearly that the geographical metaphor suits our political life because it attempts to be centralized and continuously aspires, despite the existence of distinct authorities and functions, to define or identify a centre of the centre, from which everything would start and where everything would finish. Obviously it is not simply a question of metaphor when people wonder, as they sometimes do, whether the centre of power is shifting from the Elysée to Matignon or even from Matignon to the Palais-Royal (where the Constitutional Council sits): and we may justly ask ourselves whether the consistently tense and turbulent nature of French democratic life does not result partly from the tension between a political ideal of plurality, democracy and balance (on which everyone is in theoretical agreement) and an intellectual, geographico-political model of government inherited from history (which is not very compatible with this ideal, and which perpetually incites the French to rethink its basic principles and redefine its centre).

On the geographical level, then, those Parisians – not the most numerous group – who still have time to stroll about could experience the centre of Paris as an itinerary following the course of the Seine, plied by river steamers from which most of the capital's historical and political monuments can be seen. But there are other centres identified with squares, with crossroads in which monuments are placed (Etoile, Concorde), with monuments themselves (the Opéra, the Madeleine) or with the roads leading to them (avenue de l'Opéra, rue de la Paix, Champs-Elysées), as if everything in the capital of France had to become a centre and a monument. Indeed, this process is still going on, even though the specific characters of the different *arrondissements* are fading away at the same time. We know that each of these used to have its own character, that the clichés in songs about Paris are not without foundation; and it would certainly still be possible in our time to make a detailed description of the *arrondissements*, their activities, their 'personalities' in the sense in which American anthropologists have used the term, but also of their transformations and the movements of population which are altering their ethnic or social make-up. Léo Malet's detective thrillers, many of which are set in the fourteenth and fifteenth *arrondissements*, hark back nostalgically to the 1950s, but are still not wholly out of date.

All the same, people live less and less in Paris (although they still work there a lot), and this change appears to be the sign of a more general mutation in our country. Perhaps the relationship with history that haunts our landscapes is being aestheticized, and at the same time desocialized and artificialized. Certainly, we all commemorate Hugues Capet and the Revolution of 1789 in the same spirit; we are still capable of confronting each other fiercely over differences in our relations with our common past and the contradictory interpretations of events which have marked it. But, since Malraux, our towns have been turning into museums (restored, exposed and floodlit monuments, listed areas, pedestrian precincts) while at the same time bypasses, motorways, high-speed trains and one-way systems have made it unnecessary for us to linger in them.

But this turning away, this bypassing, is not without some feeling of remorse, as we can see from the numerous signboards inviting us not to ignore the splendours of the area and its traces of history. Paradoxically, it is at the city limits, in the cold, gloomy space of big housing schemes, industrial zones and supermarkets, that the signs are placed inviting us to visit the ancient monuments; and alongside the motorways that we see more and more references to the local curiosities we ought to stop and examine, instead of just rushing past; as if alluding to former times and places were today just a manner of talking about present space.

From Places to
Non-Places

The presence of the past in a present that supersedes it
but still lays claim to it: it is in this reconciliation that
Jean Starobinski sees the essence of modernity. In a
recent article he points out in this connection that
certain authors, indubitably representative of modernity in art, outlined

> the possibility of a polyphony in which the virtually in-
> finite interlacing of destinies, actions, thoughts and rem-
> iniscences would rest on a bass line that chimed the hours
> of the terrestrial day, and marked the position that used to
> be (and could still be) occupied there by ancient ritual.

He quotes the first pages of Joyce's *Ulysses*, containing
the words of the liturgy: '*Introibo ad altare Dei*'; the

beginning of *Remembrance of Things Past*, where the cycle of the hours around the Combray bell tower punctuates the rhythm 'of a vast and solitary bourgeois day'; and Claude Simon's *Histoire*, in which

> memories of religious school, the Latin prayer in the morning, grace at midday, the evening Angelus, provide landmarks amid the views, the disassembled schemes, the quotations of all sorts that stem from every period of existence, from the imagination and the historical past, proliferating in apparent disorder around a central secret . . . .

These 'premodern figures of continuous temporality, which the modern writer tries to show he has not forgotten even as he is becoming free of them' are also specific spatial figures from a world which since the Middle Ages, as Jacques Le Goff has shown, had built itself around its church and bell tower by reconciling a recentred space with a reordered time. Starobinski's article begins significantly with a quotation from the first poem in Baudelaire's *Tableaux parisiens*, where the spectacle of modernity brings together in a single poetic flight:

> *. . . the workshop with its song and chatter;*
> *Chimneys and spires, those masts of the city,*
> *And the great skies making us dream of eternity.*

'Bass line': the expression Starobinski employs to evoke ancient places and rhythms is significant: modernity does not obliterate them but pushes them into the background. They are like gauges indicating the passage and continuation of time. They survive like the words that express them and will express them in future. Modernity in art preserves all the temporalities of place, the ones that are located in space and in words.

Behind the cycle of the hours and the outstanding features of the landscape, what we find are words and languages: the specialized words of the liturgy, of 'ancient ritual', in contrast to the 'song and chatter' of the workshop; and the words, too, of all who speak the same language, and thus recognize that they belong to the same world. Place is completed through the word, through the allusive exchange of a few passwords between speakers who are conniving in private complicity. Vincent Descombes writes of Proust's Françoise that she defines a 'rhetorical' territory shared with everyone who is capable of following her reasoning, those whose aphorisms, vocabulary and modes of thought form a 'cosmology': what the narrator of *Things Past* calls the 'Combray philosophy'.

If a place can be defined as relational, historical and concerned with identity, then a space which cannot be defined as relational, or historical, or concerned with identity will be a non-place. The hypothesis advanced here is that supermodernity produces non-places, meaning spaces which are not themselves anthropological places and which, unlike Baudelairean modernity, do not integrate the earlier places: instead these are listed, classified, promoted to the status of 'places of memory', and assigned to a circumscribed and specific position. A world where people are born in the clinic and die in hospital, where transit points and temporary abodes are proliferating under luxurious or inhuman conditions (hotel chains and squats, holiday clubs and refugee camps, shantytowns threatened with demolition or doomed to festering longevity); where a dense network of means of transport which are also inhabited spaces is developing; where the habitué of supermarkets, slot machines and credit cards communicates wordlessly, through gestures, with an abstract, unmediated commerce; a world thus surrendered to solitary individuality, to the fleeting, the temporary and ephemeral, offers the anthropologist (and others) a new object, whose unprecedented dimensions might usefully be measured before we start wondering to what sort of gaze it may be amenable. We should add that the same things apply to the non-place as to the place. It never exists in pure form; places reconstitute themselves in it; relations are restored and resumed in it; the 'millennial ruses' of 'the invention of the everyday' and 'the arts of doing', so subtly analysed by Michel de Certeau, can clear a path there and deploy their strategies. Place and non-place are rather like opposed polarities: the first is never completely erased, the second never totally completed; they are like palimpsests on which the scrambled game of identity and relations is ceaselessly rewritten. But non-places are the real measure of our time; one that could be quantified – with the aid of a few conversions between area, volume and distance – by totalling all the air, rail and motorway routes, the mobile cabins called 'means of transport' (aircraft, trains and road vehicles), the airports and railway stations, hotel chains, leisure parks, large retail outlets, and finally the complex skein of cable and wireless networks that mobilize extraterrestrial space for the purposes of a communication so peculiar that it often puts the individual in contact only with another image of himself.

The distinction between places and non-places derives from the opposition between place and space. An essential preliminary here is the analysis of the notions of place and space suggested by Michel de Certeau. He himself does not oppose 'place' and 'space' in the way that 'place' is opposed to 'non-place'. Space, for him, is a 'frequented place', 'an intersection of moving bodies': it is the pedestrians who transform a street (geometrically defined as a

place by town planners) into a space. This parallel
between the place as an assembly of elements coexisting in a certain order and the space as animation of
these places by the motion of a moving body is backed
by several references that define its terms. The first of
these references (p. 173) is to Merleau-Ponty who, in
his *Phénoménologie de la perception*, draws a distinction
between 'geometric' space and 'anthropological space'
in the sense of 'existential' space, the scene of an
experience of relations with the world on the part of
a being essentially situated 'in relation to a milieu'.
The second reference is to words and the act of
locution:

> The space could be to the place what the word becomes
> when it is spoken: grasped in the ambiguity of being
> accomplished, changed into a term stemming from mul-
> tiple conventions, uttered as the act of one present (or
> one time), and modified by the transformations resulting
> from successive influences . . . . (p. 173)

The third reference, which stems from the second,
highlights the narrative as an effort that ceaselessly
'transforms places into spaces and spaces into places'
(p. 174). There follows, naturally, a distinction
between 'doing' and 'seeing', observable in everyday
language which by turns suggests a picture ('there
is . . .') and organizes movements ('you go in, you

cross, you turn . . .'), or in map signs: from medieval maps, essentially comprising the outlines of routes and itineraries, to more recent maps from which 'route describers' have disappeared and which display, on the basis of 'elements of disparate origins', an 'inventory' of geographical knowledge. Lastly, the narrative, and especially the journey narrative, is compatible with the double necessity of 'doing' and 'seeing' ('histories of journeys and actions are punctuated by the mention of the places resulting from them or authorizing them', p. 177) but is ultimately associated with what Certeau calls 'delinquency' because it 'crosses', 'transgresses' and endorses 'the privileging of the route over the inventory' (p. 190).

A few terminological definitions are needed at this point. Place, as defined here, is not quite the place Certeau opposes to space (in the same way that the geometrical figure is opposed to movement, the unspoken to the spoken word or the inventory to the route): it is place in the established and symbolized sense, anthropological place. Naturally, this sense has to be put to work, the place has to come to life and journeys have to be made, and there is nothing to forbid the use of the word space to describe this movement. But that is not what we are saying here: we include in the notion of anthropological place the possibility of the journeys made in it, the discourses uttered in it, and the language characterizing it. And the notion of space, in the way it is used at present (to talk about the conquest of outer space, in terms which, for the time being, are more functional than lyrical, or to designate unnamed or hard-to-name places as well as possible, or with the minimum of inaccuracy, in the recent but already stereotyped language of travel, hotel and leisure institutions: 'leisure spaces', 'sports spaces', rather like 'rendezvous point'), seems to apply usefully, through the very fact of its lack of characterization, to the non-symbolized surfaces of the planet.

As a result, we might be tempted to contrast the symbolized space of place with the non-symbolized space of non-place. But this would hold us to the existing negative definition of non-places, which Michel de Certeau's analysis of the notion of space may help us to improve upon.

The term 'space' is more abstract in itself than the term 'place', whose usage at least refers to an event (which has taken place), a myth (said to have taken place) or a history (high places). It is applied in much the same way to an area, a distance between two things or points (a two-metre 'space' is left between the posts of a fence) or to a temporal expanse ('in the space of a week'). It is thus eminently abstract, and it is significant that it should be in systematic if still somewhat differentiated use today, in current speech and in the specific language of various institutions representative of our time. The *Grand Larousse illustré* makes a separate case of 'airspace', which designates that part of the atmosphere in which a state controls the air traffic (less concrete, however, than its maritime equivalent, 'territorial waters'), but also cites other uses which testify to the term's plasticity. In the expression 'European judicial space' it is clear that the notion of frontier is implied but that, setting aside this notion of frontier, what is expressed is a whole institutional and normative mass which cannot be localized. The expression 'advertising space' applies either to an area or to a length of time 'set aside for advertising in the various media'; 'buying space' refers to all the 'operations carried out by an advertising agency in connection with advertising space'. The craze for the word 'space', applied indiscriminately to auditoriums or meeting-rooms ('Espace Cardin' in Paris, 'Espace Yves Rocher' at La Gacilly), parks or gardens ('green space'), aircraft seats ('Espace 2000') and cars (Renault 'Espace'), expresses not only the themes that haunt the contemporary era (advertising, image, leisure, freedom, travel) but also the abstraction that corrodes and threatens them, as if the consumers of contemporary space were invited first and foremost to treat themselves to words.

To frequent space, Michel de Certeau writes, is 'to repeat the gleeful and silent experience of infancy: to be other, and go over to the other, in a place' (p. 164).

The gleeful and silent experience of infancy is that of
the first journey, of birth as the primal experience of
differentiation, of recognition of the self as self and as
other, repeated later in the experiences of walking as
the first use of space, and of the mirror as the first
identification with the image of the self. All narrative
goes back to infancy. When he uses the expression
'space narratives', de Certeau means both the narratives that 'traverse' and 'organize' places ('Every
narrative is a journey narrative . . .', p. 171) and the
place that is constituted by the writing of the narrative
('. . . reading is the space produced by frequentation
of the place constituted by a system of signs – a
narrative', p. 173). But the book is written before
being read; it passes through different places before
becoming one itself: like the journey, the narrative
that describes it traverses a number of places. This
plurality of places, the demands it makes on the
powers of observation and description (the impossi-
bility of seeing everything or saying everything), and
the resulting feeling of 'disorientation' (but only a
temporary one: 'This is me in front of the Parthenon,'
you will say later, forgetting that when the photo was
taken you were wondering what on earth you were
doing there), causes a break or discontinuity between
the spectator–traveller and the space of the landscape
he is contemplating or rushing through. This prevents
him from perceiving it as a place, from being fully

present in it, even though he may try to fill the gap with comprehensive and detailed information out of guidebooks . . . or journey narratives.

When Michel de Certeau mentions 'non-place', it is to allude to a sort of negative quality of place, an absence of the place from itself, caused by the name it has been given. Proper names, he tells us, impose on the place 'an injunction coming from the other (a history . . .)'. It is certainly true that someone who, in describing a route, states the names appearing along it, does not necessarily know much about the places. But can a name alone be sufficient to produce 'this erosion or non-place, gouged' out of a place 'by the law of the other' (p. 159)? Every itinerary, Michel de Certeau says, is in a sense 'diverted' by names which give it 'meanings (or directions) that could not have been predicted in advance'. And he adds: 'These names create non-place in the places; they turn them into passages' (p. 156). We could say, conversely, that the act of passing gives a particular status to place names, that the faultline resulting from the law of the other, and causing a loss of focus, is the horizon of every journey (accumulation of places, negation of place), and that the movement that 'shifts lines' and traverses places is, by definition, creative of itineraries: that is, words and non-places.

Space, as frequentation of *places* rather than a place, stems in effect from a double movement: the traveller's movement, of course, but also a parallel movement of the landscapes which he catches only in partial glimpses, a series of 'snapshots' piled hurriedly into his memory and, literally, recomposed in the account he gives of them, the sequencing of slides in the commentary he imposes on his entourage when he returns. Travel (something the ethnologist mistrusts to the point of 'hatred'[5]) constructs a fictional relationship between gaze and landscape. And while we use the word 'space' to describe the frequentation of *places* which specifically defines the journey, we should still remember that there are spaces in which the individual feels himself to be a spectator without paying much attention to the spectacle. As if the position of spectator were the essence of the spectacle, as if basically the spectator in the position of a spectator were his own spectacle. A lot of tourism leaflets suggest this deflection, this reversal of the gaze, by offering the would-be traveller advance images of curious or contemplative faces, solitary or in groups, gazing across infinite oceans, scanning ranges of snow-capped mountains or wondrous urban skylines: his own image in a word, his anticipated image, which speaks only about him but carries another name (Tahiti, Alpe d'Huez, New York). The traveller's space may thus be the archetype of *non-place*.

---

5. 'Je haïs les voyages et les explorations . . .' (Claude Lévi-Strauss, *Tristes Tropiques*). [Tr.]

To the coexistence of worlds, and the combined experience of anthropological place and something which is no longer anthropological place (in substance Starobinski's definition of modernity), movement adds the particular experience of a form of solitude and, in the literal sense, of 'taking up a position': the experience of someone who, confronted with a landscape he ought to contemplate, cannot avoid contemplating, 'strikes the pose' and derives from his awareness of this attitude a rare and sometimes melancholy pleasure. Thus it is not surprising that it is among solitary 'travellers' of the last century – not professional travellers or scientists, but travellers on impulse or for unexpected reasons – that we are most likely to find prophetic evocations of spaces in which neither identity, nor relations, nor history really make any sense; spaces in which solitude is experienced as an overburdening or emptying of individuality, in which only the movement of the fleeting images enables the observer to hypothesize the existence of a past and glimpse the possibility of a future.

Even more than Baudelaire (who derived satisfaction from the mere urge to travel) one thinks at this point of Chateaubriand, who travelled incessantly, who knew how to see, but who saw mainly the death of civilizations, the destruction or degradation of once-glittering landscapes, the disappointing shards of crumbled monuments. Vanished Sparta, ruined

Greece occupied by an invader wholly ignorant of its ancient splendours, conjured up before the 'passing' traveller a simultaneous image of lost history and life passing by, but it was the journey's movement itself that seduced him and drew him on. A movement whose only end was itself, unless it was the writing that fixed and reiterated its image.

Everything is clearly stated from the beginning of the first preface to *Itinéraire de Paris à Jérusalem*. In it Chateaubriand denies having made the journey 'to write about it', but admits that he used it to look for 'images' for *Les Martyrs*. He has no scientific pretensions: 'I make no attempt to follow the footsteps of people like Chardin, Tavernier, Chandler, Mungo Park, Humboldt . . .' (p. 19). So that finally this work, for which no purpose is admitted, answers a contradictory desire to speak of nothing but its author without saying a single thing about him to anyone:

> For the rest, it is the man, much more than the author, who will be seen throughout; I speak eternally about myself, and did so in all confidence, since I had no intention of publishing my Memoirs. (p. 20)

The vantage points favoured by the visitor and described by the writer are evidently the ones from which a series of remarkable features can be seen ('. . . Mount Hymettus to the east, Mount Pantelicus to the north, the Parnes to the north-west . . .'), but the contemplation ends, significantly, the moment it turns back on itself, becomes its own object, and seems to dissolve under the vague multitude of similar views from the past and still to come:

> This picture of Attica, the spectacle I was contemplating, had been contemplated by eyes that closed for the last time two thousand years ago. I too will pass on when my turn comes: other men as fleeting as myself will one day have the same thoughts on the same ruins . . . (p. 153)

The ideal vantage point – because it combines the effect of movement with distance – is the deck of a ship putting out to sea. A description of the vanishing land is sufficient to evoke the passenger still straining to see it: soon it is only a shadow, a rumour, a noise. This abolition of place is also the consummation of the journey, the traveller's last pose:

> As we drew away, the columns of Sunium showed more beautifully above the waves: they could be seen perfectly against the azure of the sky because of their extreme whiteness and the balminess of the night. Already we were quite far from the cape, although our ears were still struck by the seething of the waves at the foot of the rock, the murmur of the wind in the

junipers, and the song of the crickets which today alone inhabit the temple ruins: these were the last sounds that I heard in the land of Greece. (p. 190)

Whatever he may claim ('I shall perhaps be the last Frenchman to leave my country for travels in the Holy Land with the ideas, the purpose and the feelings of an ancient pilgrim', p. 133), Chateaubriand was not on a pilgrimage. The high point at the end of the pilgrimage is, by definition, overloaded with meaning. The meaning people seek there is worth the same to the individual pilgrim today that it always was. The itinerary leading to it, dotted with stages and high spots, comprises with it a 'one-way' place, a 'space' in the sense employed by Michel de Certeau. Alphonse Dupront points out that the sea crossing itself has an initiatory value here:

Thus, on pilgrimage routes, when a crossing is necessary, there is a discontinuity and, as it were, a banalization of heroism. Land and water are very unequal in showing people at their best, and above all sea crossings cause a break imposed by the mysteriousness of water. Behind these apparent facts was hidden another, deeper reality, which seems to have been perceived intuitively by certain early-twelfth-century churchmen: that of the completion, through a sea journey, of a rite of passage. (p. 31)

Chateaubriand's case is another thing entirely; his ultimate destination was not Jerusalem but Spain, where
he planned to join his mistress (the *Itinéraire* is not a
confession, though: Chateaubriand shows discretion
and 'maintains the pose'). And he finds the holy places
less than inspiring. Too much has already been written
about them:

> . . . Here I experience a difficulty. Should I produce an
> exact portrait of the holy places? But then I could only
> repeat what has already been said: never perhaps has
> there been a subject so little known to modern readers,
> yet never was any subject more completely exhausted.
> Should I omit the picture of these holy places? But
> would not that be to remove the most essential part of
> my voyage, to deprive it of what is its end and purpose?
> (p. 308)

Doubtless, too, the Christian he would like to be cannot celebrate the relentless decline of all things quite
so glibly in these places as he does when he gazes
across Attica and Sparta. Instead he resorts to assiduous
description, makes a show of erudition, quotes whole
pages of travellers or poets like Milton or Tasso. What
he is doing here is *being evasive*, and the abundance of
verbiage and documentation really does make it possible to identify Chateaubriand's holy places as a
non-place, very similar to the ones outlined in pictures

and slogans by our guidebooks and brochures. If we turn for a moment to the definition of modernity as the willed coexistence of two different worlds (Baudelairean modernity), we can see that the experience of non-place as a turning back on the self, a simultaneous distancing from the spectator and the spectacle, is not always absent from it. Starobinski, commenting on the first poem of the *Tableaux parisiens*, insists that it is the coexistence of two worlds, chimneys alongside spires, that makes the modern town; but that it also locates the particular position of the poet who, broadly speaking, wants to see things from high up and far away, and belongs neither to the universe of religion nor to that of labour. For Starobinski, this position corresponds to the double aspect of modernity: 'Loss of the subject among the crowd – or, inversely, absolute power, claimed by the individual consciousness.'

But it can also be said that the position of the poet in the act of looking is a spectacle in itself. In this Parisian tableau, it is Baudelaire who occupies the central position, the one from which he sees the town but which another self, at a distance, makes the object of a 'second sight':

> *Chin on my two hands, from my mansarded eyrie,*
> *I shall see the workshop with its song and chatter,*
> *Chimneys, spires . . .*

Here Baudelaire is not just referring to the necessary coexistence of ancient religion and new industry, or the absolute power of individual consciousness, but describing a very particular and modern form of solitude. The spelling out of a position, a 'posture', an attitude in the most physical and commonplace sense of the term, comes at the end of a movement that empties the landscape, and the gaze of which it is the object, of all content and all meaning, precisely because the gaze dissolves into the landscape and becomes the object of a secondary, unattributable gaze – the same one, or another.

In my opinion these shifts of gaze and plays of imagery, this emptying of the consciousness, can be caused – this time in systematic, generalized and prosaic fashion – by the characteristic features of what I have proposed to call 'supermodernity'. These subject the individual consciousness to entirely new experiences and ordeals of solitude, directly linked with the appearance and proliferation of non-places. But before going on to examine the non-places of supermodernity in detail, it may be useful to mention, albeit allusively, the attitudes displayed by the most recognized representatives of artistic 'modernity' in relation to the notions of place and space. We know that Benjamin's interest in Parisian 'passages' and, more generally, in iron and glass architecture, stems partly from the fact that he sees these things as embodying a wish to prefigure the architecture of the next century, as a dream or anticipation. By the same token, we may wonder whether yesterday's representatives of modernity, who found material for reflection in the world's concrete space, might not have illuminated in advance certain aspects of today's supermodernity; not through the accident of a few lucky intuitions, but because they already embodied in an exceptional way (because they were artists) situations (postures, attitudes) which, in more prosaic form, have now become the common lot.

Clearly the word 'non-place' designates two complementary but distinct realities: spaces formed in relation to certain ends (transport, transit, commerce, leisure), and the relations that individuals have with these spaces. Although the two sets of relations overlap to a large extent, and in any case officially (individuals travel, make purchases, relax), they are still not confused with one another; for non-places mediate a whole mass of relations, with the self and with others, which are only indirectly connected with their purposes. As anthropological places create the organically social, so non-places create solitary contractuality. Try to imagine a Durkheimian analysis of a transit lounge at Roissy!

The link between individuals and their surroundings in the space of non-place is established through the mediation of words, or even texts. We know, for a start, that there are words that make image – or rather, images: the imagination of a person who has never been to Tahiti or Marrakesh takes flight the moment these names are read or heard. Hence the TV game shows that derive so much of their popularity from giving rich prizes of travel and accommodation ('a week for two at a three-star hotel in Morocco', 'a fortnight's full board in Florida'): the mere mention of the prizes is sufficient to give pleasure to viewers who have never won them and never will. The 'weight of words' (a source of pride to one French weekly, which backs it up with 'the impact of photos') is not restricted to proper names; a number of common nouns (holiday, voyage, sea, sun, cruise . . .) some-times, in certain contexts, possess the same evocative force. It is easy to imagine the attraction that might have been and may still be exercised, elsewhere and in the opposite direction, by words we find less exotic, or even devoid of the slightest effect of distance: America, Europe, West, consumption, traffic. Certain places exist only through the words that evoke them, and in this sense they are non-places, or rather, imag-inary places: banal utopias, clichés. They are the opposite of Michel de Certeau's non-place. Here the word does not create a gap between everyday func-tionality and lost myth: it creates the image, produces the myth and at the same stroke makes it work (TV viewers watch the programme every week, Albanians camp in Italy dreaming of America, tourism expands).

But the real non-places of supermodernity – the ones we inhabit when we are driving down the motorway, wandering through the supermarket or sitting in an airport lounge waiting for the next flight to London or Marseille – have the peculiarity that they are defined partly by the words and texts they offer us: their 'instructions for use', which may be prescriptive ('Take right-hand lane'), prohibitive ('No smoking') or informative ('You are now entering the Beaujolais region'). Sometimes these are couched in more or less explicit and codified ideograms (on road signs, maps and tourist guides), sometimes in ordinary language. This establishes the traffic conditions of spaces in which individuals are supposed to interact only with texts, whose proponents are not individuals but 'moral entities' or institutions (airports, airlines, Ministry of Transport, commercial companies, traffic police, municipal councils); sometimes their presence is explicitly stated ('this road section financed by the General Council', 'the state is working to improve your living conditions'), sometimes it is only vaguely discernible behind the injunctions, advice, commentaries and 'messages' transmitted by the innumerable 'supports' (signboards, screens, posters) that form an integral part of the contemporary landscape.

France's well-designed autoroutes reveal landscapes somewhat reminiscent of aerial views, very different from the ones seen by travellers on the old national and departmental main roads. They represent, as it were, a change from intimist cinema to the big sky of Westerns. But it is the texts planted along the wayside that tell us about the landscape and make its secret beauties explicit. Main roads no longer pass through towns, but lists of their notable features – and, indeed, a whole commentary – appear on big signboards nearby. In a sense the traveller is absolved of the need to stop or even look. Thus, drivers batting down the *autoroute du sud* are urged to pay attention to a thirteenth-century fortified village, a renowned vineyard, the 'eternal hill' of Vézelay, the landscapes of the Avallonnais and even those of Cézanne (the return of culture into a nature which is concealed, but still talked about). The landscape keeps its distance, but its natural or architectural details give rise to a text, sometimes supplemented by a schematic plan when it appears that the passing traveller is not really in a position to see the remarkable feature drawn to his attention, and thus has to derive what pleasure he can from the mere knowledge of its proximity.

Motorway travel is thus doubly remarkable: it avoids, for functional reasons, all the principal places to which it takes us; and it makes comments on them. Service stations add to this information, adopting an increasingly aggressive role as centres of regional culture, selling a range of local goods with a few maps and guidebooks that might be useful to anyone who is thinking of stopping. Of course the fact is that most of those who pass by do not stop; but they may pass by again, every summer or several times a year, so that an abstract space, one they have regular occasion to read rather than see, can become strangely familiar to them over time; much as other, richer people get used to the orchid-seller at Bangkok airport, or the duty-free shop at Roissy I.

In the France of thirty years ago, the *routes nationales*, departmental main roads and railways used to penetrate the intimacy of everyday life. The difference between road and rail routes, from this point of view, was like the difference between the front and back of something; the same difference is still partially perceptible today to anyone who keeps to departmental main roads and the railways (TGV excepted), especially regional lines (where they still exist, for significantly it is the *local* services, the roads of *local* interest, that are vanishing fastest). Departmental roads, which today are often rerouted to bypass towns and villages, used to pass through their main streets, lined with houses on both sides. Before eight o'clock in the morning or after seven at night, the traveller would drive through a desert of blank façades (shutters closed, chinks of light filtering through the slats, but only sometimes, since bedrooms and living-rooms usually faced the back of the house): he was witness to the worthy, contained image the French like to give of themselves, that every Frenchman likes to project to his neighbours. The passing motorist used to see something of towns which today have become names on a route (La Ferté-Bernard, Nogent-le-Rotrou); the texts he might happen to decipher (shop signs, municipal edicts) during a traffic hold-up, or while waiting at a red light, were not addressed primarily to him. Trains, on the other hand, were – and remain – more indiscreet. The railway, which often passes behind the houses making up the town, catches provincials off guard in the privacy of their daily lives, behind the façade, on the garden side, the kitchen or bedroom side and, in the evening, the light side (while the street, if it were not for public street lighting, would be the domain of darkness and night). Trains used to go slowly enough for the curious traveller to be able to read the names on passing stations, but this is made impossible by the excessive speed of today's trains. It is as if certain texts had become obsolete for the contemporary passenger. He is offered others: on the aircraft-like train the TGV has become, he can leaf through a magazine rather like the ones provided by airlines for their passengers: it reminds him, in articles, photos and advertisements, of the need to live on the scale (or in the image) of today's world.

Another example of the invasion of space by text is the big supermarket. The customer wanders round in silence, reads labels, weighs fruit and vegetables on a machine that gives the price along with the weight; then hands his credit card to a young woman as silent as himself – anyway, not very chatty – who runs each article past the sensor of a decoding machine before checking the validity of the customer's credit card. There is a more direct but even more silent dialogue between the cardholder and the cash dispenser: he inserts the card, then reads the instructions on its screen, generally encouraging in tone but sometimes including phrases ('Card faulty', 'Please withdraw your card', 'Read instructions carefully') that call him rather sternly to order. All the remarks that emanate from our roads and commercial centres, from the street-corner sites of the vanguard of the banking system ('Thank you for your custom', 'Bon voyage', 'We apologize for any inconvenience') are addressed simultaneously and indiscriminately to each and any of us: they fabricate the 'average man', defined as the user of the road, retail or banking system. They fabricate him, and may sometimes individualize him: on some roads and motorways a driver who presses on too hard is recalled to order by the sudden flashing (110! 110!) of a warning sign; at some Paris junctions, cars that jump red lights are photographed automatically. Every credit card carries an identification code enabling the dispenser to provide its holder with information at the same time as a reminder of the rules of the game:

'You may withdraw 600 francs.' 'Anthropological place' is formed by individual identities, through complicities of language, local references, the unformulated rules of living know-how; non-place creates the shared identity of passengers, customers or Sunday drivers. No doubt the relative anonymity that goes with this temporary identity can even be felt as a liberation, by people who, for a time, have only to keep in line, go where they are told, check their appearance. As soon as his passport or identity card has been checked, the passenger for the next flight, freed from the weight of his luggage and everyday responsibilities, rushes into the 'duty-free' space; not so much, perhaps, in order to buy at the best prices as to experience the reality of his momentary availability, his unchallengeable position as a passenger in the process of departing.

Alone, but one of many, the user of a non-place is in contractual relations with it (or with the powers that govern it). He is reminded, when necessary, that the contract exists. One element in this is the way the non-place is to be used: the ticket he has bought, the card he will have to show at the tollbooth, even the trolley he trundles round the supermarket, are all more or less clear signs of it. The contract always relates to the individual identity of the contracting party. To get into the departure lounge of an airport, a ticket – always inscribed with the passenger's name – must first be presented at the check-in desk; proof that the contract has been respected comes at the immigration desk, with simultaneous presentation of the boarding pass and an identity document: different countries have different requirements in this area (identity card, passport, passport and visa), and checks are made at departure time to ensure that these will be properly fulfilled. So the passenger accedes to his anonymity only when he has given proof of his identity; when he has countersigned (so to speak) the contract. The supermarket customer gives his identity when he pays by cheque or credit card; so does the autoroute driver who pays the toll with a card. In a way, the user of the non-place is always required to prove his innocence. Checks on the contract and the user's identity, *a priori* or *a posteriori*, stamp the space of contemporary consumption with the sign of non-place:[6] it can be entered only by the innocent. Here words hardly count any longer. There will be no individualization (no right to anonymity) without identity checks.

Of course, the criteria of innocence are the established, official criteria of individual identity (entered on cards, stored in mysterious databanks). But the

---

6. The expression *non-lieu*, which in the present text usually means 'non-place', is more commonly used in French in the technical juridicial sense of 'no case to answer' or 'no grounds for prosecution': a recognition that the accused is innocent. [Tr.]

innocence itself is something else again: a person entering the space of non-place is relieved of his usual determinants. He becomes no more than what he does or experiences in the role of passenger, customer or driver. Perhaps he is still weighed down by the previous day's worries, the next day's concerns; but he is distanced from them temporarily by the environment of the moment. Subjected to a gentle form of possession, to which he surrenders himself with more or less talent or conviction, he tastes for a while – like anyone who is possessed – the passive joys of identity-loss, and the more active pleasure of role-playing.

What he is confronted with, finally, is an image of himself, but in truth it is a pretty strange image. The only face to be seen, the only voice to be heard, in the silent dialogue he holds with the landscape-text addressed to him along with others, are his own: the face and voice of a solitude made all the more baffling by the fact that it echoes millions of others. The passenger through non-places retrieves his identity only at Customs, at the tollbooth, at the check-out counter. Meanwhile, he obeys the same code as others, receives the same messages, responds to the same entreaties. The space of non-place creates neither singular identity nor relations; only solitude, and similitude.

There is no room there for history unless it has been transformed into an element of spectacle, usually in allusive texts. What reigns there is actuality, the urgency of the present moment. Since non-places are there to be passed through, they are measured in units of time. Itineraries do not work without timetables, lists of departure and arrival times in which a corner is always found for a mention of possible delays. They are lived through in the present. The present of the journey, materialized today on long-distance flights by a screen giving minute-to-minute updates on the aircraft's progress. From time to time the flight captain makes this explicit in a somewhat redundant fashion: 'The city of Lisbon should be visible to the right of the aircraft.' Actually there is nothing to be seen: once again, the spectacle is only an idea, only a word. On the motorway, occasional luminous signs give the ambient temperature and information helpful to those frequenting the space: 'Two-kilometre tailback on A3'. This present is one of actuality in the broad sense: in aircraft, newspapers are read and reread; some airlines even retransmit TV current affairs programmes. Most cars are fitted with radios; the radio plays continuously in service stations and supermarkets: buzzwords of the day, advertisements, a few snippets of news are offered to – inflicted on – passing customers. Everything proceeds as if space had been trapped by time, as if there were no history other than the last forty-eight hours of news, as if each individual history were drawing its motives, its words and images, from the inexhaustible stock of an unending history in the present.

Assailed by the images flooding from commercial, transport or retail institutions, the passenger in non-places has the simultaneous experiences of a perpetual present and an encounter with the self. Encounter, identification, image: *he* is this well-dressed forty-year-old, apparently tasting ineffable delights under the attentive gaze of a blonde hostess; *he* is this steady-eyed rally driver hurling his turbo-diesel down some god-forsaken African back-road; and that virile-looking fellow at whom a woman is gazing amorously because he uses toilet water with a wild scent: that is him too. If these invitations to identification are essentially masculine, it is because the ego-ideal they project is masculine; at present, a credible businesswoman or woman driver is perceived as possessing 'masculine' qualities. The tone changes, naturally, in supermarkets, those less prestigious non-places where women are in a majority. Here the theme of equality (even, eventually, disappearance of the distinction) between the sexes is broached in symmetrical and inverse fashion: new fathers, we sometimes read in 'women's' magazines, take an interest in housework and enjoy looking after babies. But even in supermarkets the distant rumble of contemporary prestige is audible: media, stars, the news. For the most remarkable thing in all this remains what one might call the 'intersecting participation' of publicity and advertising apparatuses.

Commercial radio stations advertise big stores; big stores advertise commercial radio. When trips to America are on special offer at the travel agencies, the radio tells us about it. Airline company magazines advertise hotels that advertise the airline companies; the interesting thing being that all space consumers thus find themselves caught among the echoes and images of a sort of cosmology which, unlike the ones traditionally studied by ethnologists, is objectively universal, and at the same time familiar and prestigious. This has at least two results. On the one hand, these images tend to make a system; they outline a world of consumption that every individual can make his own because it buttonholes him incessantly. The temptation to narcissism is all the more seductive here in that it seems to express the common law: do as others do to be yourself. On the other hand, like all cosmologies, this new cosmology produces effects of recognition. A paradox of non-place: a foreigner lost in a country he does not know (a 'passing stranger') can feel at home there only in the anonymity of motorways, service stations, big stores or hotel chains. For him, an oil company logo is a reassuring landmark; among the supermarket shelves he falls with relief on sanitary, household or food products validated by multinational brand names. On the other hand, the countries of East Europe retain a measure of exoticism, for the simple reason that they do not yet have all the necessary means to accede to the world-wide consumption space.

★

In the concrete reality of today's world, places and spaces, places and non-places intertwine and tangle together. The possibility of non-place is never absent from any place. Place becomes a refuge to the habitué of non-places (who may dream, for example, of own-ing a second home rooted in the depths of the countryside). Places and non-places are opposed (or attracted) like the words and notions that enable us to describe them. But the fashionable words – those that did not exist thirty years ago – are associated with non-places. Thus we can contrast the realities of *transit* (transit camps or passengers in transit) with those of residence or dwelling; the *interchange* (where nobody crosses anyone else's path) with the *crossroads* (where people meet); the *passenger* (defined by his *destination*) with the *traveller* (who strolls along his *route* – signifi-cantly, the SNCF still calls its customers travellers until they board the TGV; then they become passengers), the *housing estate*[7] ('group of new dwellings', Larousse says), where people do not live together and which is

---

7. *L'ensemble.* [Tr.]

never situated in the centre of anything (big estates characterize the so-called peripheral zones or out-skirts), with the *monument* where people share and commemorate; *communication* (with its codes, images and strategies) with *language* (which is spoken).

Vocabulary has a central role here because it is what weaves the tissue of habits, educates the gaze, informs the landscape. Let us return for a moment to Vincent Descombes's proposed definition of the notion of 'rhetorical country' based on an analysis of the Combray 'philosophy', or rather, 'cosmology':

> Where is the character at home? The question bears less on a geographical territory than a rhetorical territory (rhetorical in the classical sense, as defined by the rhetorical acts: plea, accusation, eulogy, censure, rec-ommendation, warning, and so on). The character is at home when he is at ease in the rhetoric of the people with whom he shares life. The sign of being at home is the ability to make oneself understood without too much difficulty, and to follow the reasoning of others without any need for long explanations. The rhetorical country of a character ends where his interlocutors no longer understand the reasons he gives for his deeds and actions, the criticisms he makes or the enthusiasms he displays. A disturbance of rhetorical communication marks the crossing of a frontier, which should of course be envisaged as a border zone, a marchland, rather than a clearly drawn line. (p. 179)

If Descombes is right, we can conclude that in the world of supermodernity people are always, and never, at home: the frontier zones or 'marchlands' he mentions no longer open on to totally foreign worlds. Supermodernity (which stems simultaneously from the three figures of excess: overabundance of events, spatial overabundance and the individualization of references) naturally finds its full expression in non-places. Words and images in transit through non-places can take root in the – still diverse – places where people still try to construct part of their daily life. Conversely, it may happen that the non-place borrows its words from the soil, something seen on autoroutes where the 'rest areas' – the term 'area' being truly the most neutral possible, the antithesis of place – are sometimes named after some particular and mysterious attribute of the surrounding land: aire du Hibou, aire du Gîte-aux-Loups, aire de la Combe-Tourmente, aire des Croquettes . . . So we live in a world where the experience that ethnologists traditionally called 'cultural contact' has become a general phenomenon. The first problem with an ethnology of the 'here' is that it still deals with an 'elsewhere', but an 'elsewhere' that cannot be perceived as a singular and distinct (exotic) object. These multiple permeations have become apparent in language. The use of 'basic English' by communications and marketing technologies is revealing in this respect: it is less a question of the triumph of one language over the others than of the invasion of all languages by a universal vocabulary. What is significant is the need for this generalized vocabulary, not the fact that it uses English words. Linguistic enfeeblement (if that is the name we give to the decline of semantic and syntactic competence in average spoken language) is attributable more to this generalization than to subversion of one language by another.

It now becomes clear what distinguishes supermodernity from modernity as defined by Starobinski through Baudelaire. Supermodernity is not all there is to the contemporary. In the modernity of the Baudelairean landscape, on the other hand, everything is combined, everything holds together: the spires and chimneys are the 'masts of the city'. What is seen by the spectator of modernity is the interweaving of old and new. Supermodernity, though, makes the old (history) into a specific spectacle, as it does with all exoticism and all local particularity. History and exoticism play the same role in it as the 'quotations' in a written text: a status superbly expressed in travel agency catalogues. In the non-places of supermodernity, there is always a specific position (in the window, on a poster, to the right of the aircraft, on the left of the motorway) for 'curiosities' presented as such: pineapples from the Ivory Coast; Venice – city of the Doges; the Tangier Kasbah; the site of Alésia. But they play no part in any synthesis, they are not integrated with anything; they simply bear witness, during a journey, to the coexistence of distinct individualities, perceived as equivalent and unconnected. Since non-places are the space of supermodernity, supermodernity cannot aspire to the same ambitions as modernity. When individuals come together, they engender the social and organize places. But the space of supermodernity is inhabited by this contradiction: it deals only with individuals (customers, passengers, users, listeners), but they are identified (name, occupation, place of birth, address) only on entering or leaving. Since non-places are the space of supermodernity, this paradox has to be explained: it seems that the social game is being played elsewhere than in the forward posts of contemporaneity. It is in the manner of immense parentheses that non-places daily receive increasing numbers of individuals. And they are the particular target of all those whose passion for retaining or conquering territory drives them to terrorism. Airports and aircraft, big stores and railway stations have always been a favoured target for attacks (to say nothing of car bombs); doubtless for reasons of efficiency, if that is the right word. But another reason might be that, in a more or less confused way, those pursuing new socializations and localizations can see non-places only as a negation of their ideal. The non-place is the opposite of utopia: it exists, and it does not contain any organic society.

At this point we again come across something touched upon earlier: the question of politics. In an article on the state of the town,[8] Sylviane Agacinski recalls the ideal and aim of the National Convention member Anacharsis Cloots. Hostile to all 'embodied' power, he called for the death of the king. All local-ized power, all singular sovereignty, even the division of humanity into different peoples, seemed to him incompatible with the indivisible sovereignty of the human species. Seen from this point of view the cap-ital, Paris, is a privileged place only to the extent that 'an uprooted, deterritorialized thought' is privileged. 'The paradox of the seat of this abstract, universal – and perhaps not simply *bourgeois* – humanity', Agacinski writes, 'is that it is also a non-place, a nowhere, something like what Michel Foucault – who did not envisage it as including the town – called a *heterotopia*' (pp. 204–5). Today it is certainly the case that the tension between thought concerned with the universal and thought concerned with territoriality is manifest on a world scale. We have looked at this here in only one of its aspects, starting with the observation that an increasing proportion of humanity lives, at least part of the time, outside territory, with the result that the very conditions defining the empirical and the

---

8. 'La ville inquiète', *Le Temps de la réflexion*, 1987.

abstract are shifting under the influence of the three-
fold acceleration characteristic of supermodernity.

The 'out-of-place' or 'non-place' frequented by the
individual under supermodernity is not the 'non-
place' of government, with its tangle of contradictory
double necessities: to think about and locate the universal, to erase and found the local, to affirm and
challenge origins. This unthinkable aspect of power
which has always lain at the base of the social order –
when necessary by inverting, as if by an arbitrary act of
nature, the terms used for thinking about it –
undoubtedly finds a particular expression in the
revolutionary wish to think simultaneously about
authority and the universal, to challenge both despo-
tism and anarchy; but it is a more general constituent
of every localized order, which must by definition
produce a spatialized expression of authority. The
constraint that limits the thought of Anacharsis Cloots
(and sometimes gives him an appearance of 'naivety')
is that he sees the world as a place; a place belonging
to the whole human species, admittedly, but involving
the organization of a space and recognition of a centre. It is significant, incidentally, that when mention is
made these days of 'Europe of the Twelve' or the
'New World Order', the question that immediately
arises is still that of the real centre of these entities:
Brussels (not to mention Strasbourg) or Bonn (not to
jump the gun with Berlin)? New York and the UN,

or Washington and the Pentagon? Thought based on place haunts us still, and the 'resurgence' of nationalisms, which is giving it new relevance, could pass for a 'return' to the localization from which Empire, as the would-be forerunner of the human species still to come, might seem to have represented a withdrawal. But in fact the language of Empire was the same as that of the nations that reject it, perhaps because the former Empire and the new nations need to conquer modernity before moving on to supermodernity. Empire, considered as a 'totalitarian' universe, is never a non-place. On the contrary, the image associated with it is that of a universe where nobody is ever alone, where everyone is under close control, where the past as such is rejected (has been swept away). Empire, like the world of Orwell or Kafka, is not premodern but 'para-modern'; a botched modernity, in no case the successor to modernity, featuring none of the three figures of supermodernity that we have tried to define. One might even say that it is its exact negative. Blind to the acceleration of history, it rewrites it; it protects its subjects from the feeling that space is shrinking by limiting freedom of movement and information; similarly (as can clearly be seen from its bad-tempered reactions to initiatives in favour of human rights), it removes the individual reference from its ideology and takes the risk of projecting it outside its frontiers: a shimmering figure of absolute evil or supreme seductiveness. Of course the first example that springs to mind is the former Soviet Union, but there are other empires, big and small; the tendency of some of our politicians to believe that the single party and sovereign executive are a necessary preliminary to democracy in Africa and Asia is strangely reminiscent of the modes of thought whose obsolescence and intrinsically perverse character they denounce when they talk about Eastern Europe. The stumbling block to the coexistence of places and non-places will always be political. Doubtless the East European countries, and others, will find their positions in the world networks of traffic and consumption. But the extension of the non-places corresponding to them – empirically measurable and analysable non-places whose definition is primarily economic – has already overtaken the thought of politicians, who spend more and more effort wondering where they are going only because they are less and less sure where they are.

Epilogue

When an international flight crosses Saudi Arabia, the hostess announces that during the overflight the drinking of alcohol will be forbidden in the aircraft. This signifies the intrusion of territory into space. Land = society = nation = culture = religion: the equation of anthropological place, fleetingly inscribed in space. Returning after an hour or so to the non-place of space, escaping from the totalitarian constraints of place, will be just like a return to something resembling freedom.

A few years ago the talented British novelist David Lodge published a modern version of the quest for the Holy Grail, a novel set with effective humour in the cosmopolitan, international and narrow world of academic linguistic and semiological research.[9] The humour in this case is sociological: the academic world depicted is only one of the social 'networks' deployed today all over the planet, offering diverse individuals the opportunity for singular but strangely similar journeys. Knight-errantry, after all, was no different, and individual wanderings, in today's reality as in yesterday's myths, still carry expectation, if not hope.

★

Ethnology always has to deal with at least two spaces: that of the place it is studying (village, factory) and the bigger one in which this place is located, the source of influences and constraints which are not without effects on the internal play of local relations (tribe, kingdom, state). The ethnologist is thus doomed to methodological strabismus: he must lose sight neither of the immediate place in which his observation is carried out, nor of the pertinent frontiers of its external marchlands.

In the situation of supermodernity, part of this exterior is made of non-places, and parts of the non-places are made of images. Frequentation of non-places today provides an experience – without real historical

9. *Small World*, Penguin, 1985.

precedent – of solitary individuality combined with non-human mediation (all it takes is a notice or a screen) between the individual and the public authority.

The ethnologist of contemporary societies thus finds the individual presence in the surrounding universe to which, traditionally, he habitually referred the general determinants that gave meaning to particular configurations or singular accidents.

★

It would be a mistake to see this play of images as nothing but an illusion (a postmodern form of alienation). The reality of a phenomenon has never been exhaustively understood by analysing its determinants. What is significant in the experience of non-place is its power of attraction, inversely proportional to territorial attraction, to the gravitational pull of place and tradition. This is obvious in different ways in the weekend and holiday stampedes along the motorways, the difficulty experienced by traffic controllers in coping with jammed air routes, the success of the latest forms of retail distribution. But it is also apparent in certain other phenomena that might at first be attributed to the wish to defend territorial values or recover patrimonial identities. Perhaps the reason why immigrants worry settled people so much (and often so abstractly) is that they expose the relative nature of certainties inscribed in the soil: the thing that is so worrying and fascinating about the character of the immigrant is the emigrant. The state of contemporary Europe certainly forces us to envisage the 'return' of nationalisms. Perhaps, though, we should pay more attention to the aspects of this 'return' that seem essentially to express rejection of the collective order: obviously the model of national identity is available to give form to this rejection, but it is the individual image (the image of the free individual course) that animates and gives meaning to the model today, and may weaken it tomorrow.

★

In one form or another, ranging from the misery of refugee camps to the cosseted luxury of five-star hotels, some experience of non-place (indissociable from a more or less clear perception of the acceleration of history and the contraction of the planet) is today an essential component of all social existence. Hence the very particular and ultimately paradoxical character of what is sometimes regarded in the West as the fashion for 'cocooning', retreating into the self: never before have individual histories (because of their necessary relations with space, image and consumption) been so deeply entangled with general history,

history *tout court*. In this situation, any individual attitude is conceivable: flight (back home, elsewhere), fear (of the self, of others), but also intensity of experience (performance) or revolt (against established values). It is no longer possible for a social analysis to dispense with individuals, nor for an analysis of individuals to ignore the spaces through which they are in transit.

*

One day, perhaps, there will be a sign of intelligent life on another world. Then, through an effect of solidarity whose mechanisms the ethnologist has studied on a small scale, the whole terrestrial space will become a single place. Being from earth will signify something. In the meantime, though, it is far from certain that threats to the environment are sufficient to produce the same effect. The community of human destinies is experienced in the anonymity of non-place, and in solitude.

*

So there will soon be a need – perhaps there already is a need – for something that may seem a contradiction in terms: an ethnology of solitude.

A Few References

Certeau, Michel de, *L'Invention du quotidien. 1. Arts de faire* (1990 edn), Gallimard, 'Folio-Essais'.

Chateaubriand, *Itinéraire de Paris à Jérusalem* (1964 edn), Julliard.

Descombes, Vincent, *Proust, philosophie du roman*, Editions de Minuit, 1987.

Dumont, Louis, *La Tarasque*, Gallimard, 1987.

Dupront, Alphonse, *Du sacré*, Gallimard, 1987.

Furet, François, *Penser la Révolution*, Gallimard, 1978.

Hazard, Paul, *La Crise de la conscience européenne, 1680–1715*, Arthème Fayard, 1961.

Mauss, Marcel, *Sociologie et anthropologie*, PUF, 1966.

Starobinski, Jean, 'Les cheminées et les clochers', *Magazine littéraire* 280, September 1990.

A Few References

L'Autre et le semblable. Regards sur l'ethnologie des sociétés contemporaines, collected and edited by Martine Segalen, Presses du CNRS, 1989.